CLASH OF KINGS

CONTENTS

CREDITS

Rules and Scenario Development
Patrick Allen, Michael Crossman, Matt James, Jason Moorman, Chris Morris, Elliot Morrish

Additional Rules Development
Kyle Przelenski

Background
Mark Lathan, Scott H Washburn

Editing
Matt Gilbert, Rob Burman

Graphic Design
Duncan Aldis

Photography
Ben Sandum

Terrain
Author's own collection, printablescenery.com, tabletop-world.com

Playtesters

Aaron Chapman, Andrew Goodman, Andrew Whitehead, Andy Marshall, Be_____s Cowburn, Daniel Bird, Daniel King, David Symonds, Dustin Howard, Ed H_____ _____ybridge, Garrett Mercier, Geoff Holland, George Kirke, Grant Fetter, Hank Googe, Je_____ _____y Duvall, John Green Jr., Jon Gunns, Jonathon Quayle, Jose Vega, Keith Conroy, Kevin Haney, Kris Kapsner, Kyle Timberlake, Marc Taylor, Mathew Sellick, Matt Carmack, Matt Croger, Matt Gee, Matthew Curtis, Michael Clarke, Michael Crossman, Michael Pearcy, Nicholas Mikelonis, Nick Legrand, Nick Oftime, Nick Prosser, Nick Williams, Page Neo, Rashad Navidi, Richard Laking, Roger Connor, Roy Bradford McKay, Si Brand, Steven Housenick, Thomas Bandur Aleksandersen, Todd Serpico, Tom Annis, Tom Robinson, Tony Winmill, Tyler Schulz, Yan Zhi Lai

INTRODUCTION

A storm rages above the Abyss. Lightning crackles across the ominous sky and thunder rolls through the mountains and valleys of the world. Garkan the Black has brought a new wickedness into the world. But as the legions of greenskins spew forth from the depths of the hellish rent upon the face of Pannithor, a new military power stirs in the heart of the Ardovikian Plain.

Welcome to the Clash of Kings 2022. It has been two years since the launch of the third edition of Kings of War. An awful lot has happened globally in the time since!

The tournament and gaming scene took a hit due to the global pandemic but that does not seem to have prevented people playing lots of games online and (in some cases at least!) getting through their backlog of unpainted minis. Of course, most of us took the opportunity to add to the pile instead!

Now some of us are lucky enough to be getting back to gaming in real life, and tournaments are happening again, it is time for a big update to the game and the armies. The changes introduced in Halpi's Rift were a light touch but it is now time to get serious...

In this book you will find all the background and rules you need to introduce two new armies to your games of Kings of War. The Halflings get their own army having split away

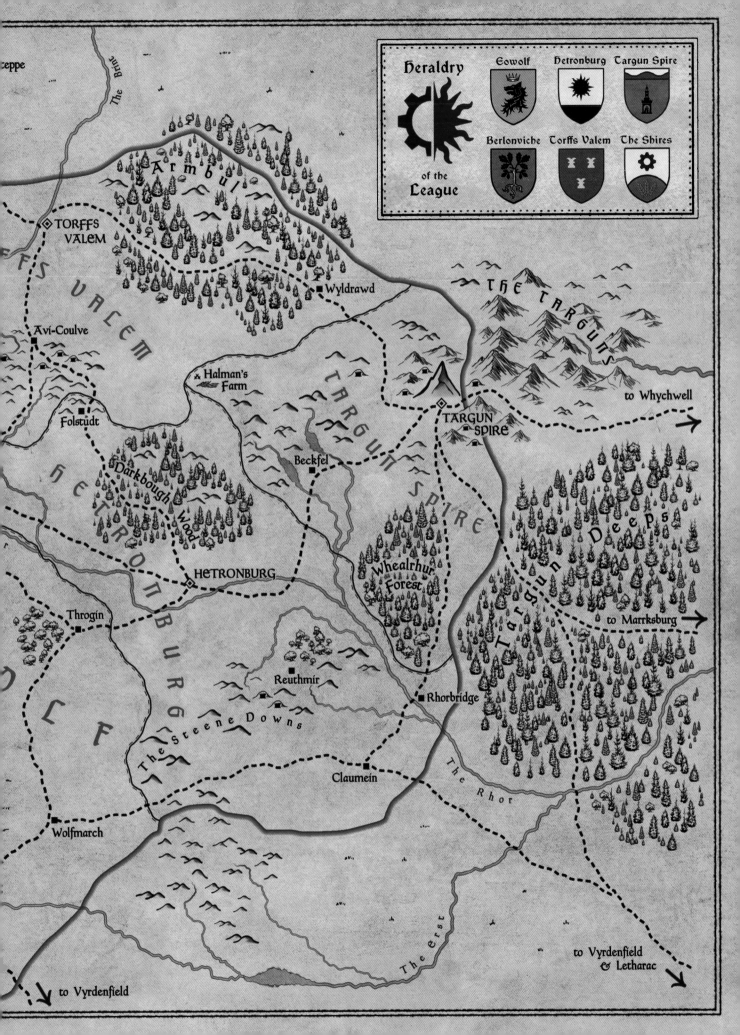

Heraldry of the League

- Eowolf
- Hetronburg
- Targun Spire
- Berlonviche
- Torffs Valem
- The Shires

to Whychwell

to Marrksburg

to Vyrdenfield & Letharac

to Vyrdenfield

Places:

- eppe
- The Brinr
- Armbul
- TORFFS VALEM
- TORFFS VALEM
- Avi-Coulve
- Folstüdt
- Halman's Farm
- Wyldrawd
- THE TARGUTS
- Targun Spire
- TARGUN SPIRE
- Darkbough Wood
- Beckfel
- HETRONBURG
- HETRONBURG
- Throgin
- Whealrhur Forest
- Targun Deeps
- Reuthmir
- OLF
- The Steene Downs
- Rhorbridge
- The Rhor
- Claumein
- Wolfmarch
- The Erst

HALFLINGS

The race of people known as the 'halflings' are, as their name would imply, rather short compared to the other peoples of Pannithor. The humans, elves, and even dwarfs are all considerably taller, although generally not twice the size. Outside the military, male halflings are typically about four feet tall, while females are a little less. They are shaped as humans, although their heads, hands, and feet are a bit larger in proportion to their height. Skin colour in the north is generally fair, but the southern halflings have a much more tanned and somewhat reddish complexion due to many generations of living in much sunnier climes. Hair colours range from black through brown, with red or blonde also seen, but not common. Beards on the males are not unknown, but most prefer to be clean shaven. Some have tufts of hair on the tops of their feet, but most wear shoes or boots so it's unclear if this is a universal trait. Halflings are not blessed with long life—the eldest recorded individual, Old Mother Chimesbury lived to the grand age of 72. Typically, most halflings live no more than into their late fifties, with perhaps the halflings of Ej living a little longer.

The halflings do not refer to themselves as such since in their eyes they are exactly the right size and it is the other races who are abnormally large. They generally just call themselves 'The People', although those who have settled in the Shires most often refer to themselves as 'Shirefolk'. Those who settled in the southern regions near and within the elven city of Ej call themselves the 'People of Ej'.

Surprisingly, even among the noble races, nothing is definitively known of the halflings' origins. Most scholars postulate that they were created by the gods after the elves, humans, and dwarfs, but no tale tells which god, when, or where. The halflings' own oral histories are vague and contradictory at best. They do not appear to worship or affiliate with any particular god or gods, but their most ancient legends say that prior to the God War the halflings did indeed have deities they revered, but the specifics are lost to the mists of time. It is theorized that whichever gods they did worship were perhaps killed during the God War or even pushed aside some time before, but the halflings, unable to conceive of a god being slain, have come to speculate that their gods simply left and are thus 'missing'. Even today, a common phrase or exclamation heard in the company of halflings is: 'missing gods.'

The first recorded mention of the halflings occurs during the years of the Grokan Dynasty, over three thousand years ago. These are brief accounts of groups of wandering nomads distinctive only due to their small stature. For the next few thousand years there are a scattering of historical notes in the dusty libraries of the world, in those that have survived from those tumultuous times. These records are all similar: beings of small stature, travelling in groups, herding sheep and goats, living in tents or hastily constructed huts. Scribbled footnotes suggest they tended to avoid other people, but would sometimes approach villages and towns to trade. The halflings' own legends simply refer to these as the 'wandering times'.

The first more detailed records of the halflings come from the dwarf archives. In the year 927, Naprastor, a chronicler in a dwarf hold on the western edges of the Mountains of Abkhazla, wrote that a detachment of rangers encountered a group of odd creatures camped on the edge of the hold's grazing lands. "Small they are," he wrote, "just a tad shorter than ourselves, but slender and gangly as are men or elves, but only half the height. They are skittish as would be expected from ones so weak and vulnerable, but became friendly enough when they realized we meant them no harm. They were eager to trade and had sheepskins and wool of very fine quality to offer. They seemed much interested in iron tools and steel blades. They live in ingeniously made dome-shaped wood and leather tents which fold up easily to be carried on pack animals, and which can be erected in moments. Our rangers were quite taken with them and traded a dozen small axes for two. A few of the creatures knew a smattering of the common tongue but they appear to have some language of their own which made no sense to us."

More accounts from dwarf, elven, and human sources record similar encounters in the following years. Several of these noted that although the halflings normally tried to avoid trouble, if forced to fight they did so with an unexpected ferocity. So much so that one human record dubbed them 'The Wolverine People'. Nearly all the accounts noted that the halflings were shrewd traders.

Spread of the halflings

It was during the second millennium after the God War that the halflings adopted wide-scale use of both the wheel and writing, apparently learned from the elves, and gleaned from the dwarfs whose engineering they appeared to admire. The increased use of the wheel resulted in the halflings developing small carts and then larger wagons. At first they traded to get ready-made wheels, but soon achieved the means to make their own. Indeed this is when the halfling's well-known penchant for tinkering and crafting began. The wagons allowed the halflings to acquire more material possessions and trade goods. The wagons often replaced the tents as living spaces and in times of danger the halflings would park the wagons in a circle, creating a ready-made fortified village. Their herds now included ponies, cattle, and oxen to haul their wagons. Most of their crafts were of wood or linen at this time as their wandering lifestyle made crafting metal difficult. Halflings had therefore traditionally acquired most of their metal tools and weapons through trade. Rapid learners, halflings seemed to have an innate talent for tools and figuring out how things worked and so it's no surprise that they began to have a reputation for ingenuity and tinkering.

Initially, their written works seem to have been limited to business dealings and from the start all halfling records were written in the common tongue. Their native language, which they referred to as Tinker-tongue has remained in usage even to the present day, but there are few written examples of it that have been found.

The early records of halfling encounters mention only small groups of a few score which seemed to be extended families. But as time went by, larger groups were observed and on occasion several of these groups would come together and establish camps which remained in one spot for weeks or months before moving on again. These gatherings were for trade, sport, and celebration, and often to allow young people to find spouses outside their immediate family. As halfling numbers increased, these gatherings became more common and would often take place near human or elf or dwarf settlements where trading on a large scale would occur. For the most part, halfling relations with the other civilised races were cordial and their goods, especially handicrafts, were welcome nearly everywhere. The other races often seemed to regard the halflings with amusement. What conflicts which did occur were usually over the use of grazing lands and water supplies and this would often force the halflings to move on sooner than they desired.

Conflict with uncivilised creatures was a far more serious matter, of course. While halflings could usually hold their own against small groups of goblins, or human bandits who foolishly thought the halflings easy prey, their only hope against larger monsters was to flee or hide—something at which they were quite adept.

Contacts with other civilised races gradually increased the halflings' interest in large scale agricultural methods. They had a natural knack for growing things, but their nomadic lifestyle made it difficult to plant crops. Early in the second millennium halflings began setting up semi-permanent camps in secluded areas where crops would be planted for a season or two. If nothing disturbed them, they might extend their stay to a year or more before moving on.

Establishment of the Shires

In 2180 a large gathering of halflings came together under the direction of Bron Abbet, the leader of one of the larger clans. They met on the Ardovikian Plain in the lands to the north and west of the recently founded League of Rhordia. Abbet declared that he and his family were tired of the endless wandering. The land there was rich and fertile and nearly unoccupied. Abbet stated his intent to found a permanent settlement and invited the others to join him. There was a great deal of debate over such a radical idea, but in the end, the majority of the families agreed to stay. A region was staked out and named Abbetshire. The chief settlement was made near a lake and named Yangmere—which in Tinker-tongue simply meant 'Laketown'.

Word of this quickly spread among the other halfling families in the region but most took a wait-and-see attitude at first. But after a dozen years without disaster befalling the settlers, many began to flock to Abbetshire and the population grew rapidly and other communities were founded. Countless years collating and subsuming all the knowledge of the peoples they had met on their travels began to pay off, and the accumulated wisdom was put to good use. At last able to make full use of their agricultural skills, Abbetshire was soon growing more food than was needed locally and trade was quickly established with surrounding human settlements, especially the nearby League of Rhordia.

With the passage of time, more and more of the wandering halflings were drawn to Abbetshire, although a few retained their traditional nomadic lifestyle, and even still do to the present day, either in small groups or in larger, travelling families. As the population grew and more land was cultivated, the halflings spread out and ultimately established four more shires: Tanshire, Daleshire, Southshire, and Hoddingshire, covering an area about sixty miles east to west and sixty-five north to south. It should be noted that while these lands were sparsely inhabited by local humans, they were not uninhabited. The halflings proved to be rather ruthless in evicting these people, and creatures, and making sure no more tried to settle in lands they now considered their own.

Government

Historically, the halflings had lived in family groups with the eldest family member, male or female, establishing the rules and making the decisions. If a group became too large to be supported by the land they could graze, the group would split, but the family ties were remembered. If the groups came together again to trade or during one of the gatherings, the eldest member would have authority over the whole group, or clan as it was called.

When the halflings settled permanently in the Shires, a different social structure developed. At first, Bron Abbet was acknowledged as the leader, but after his death no one accepted the idea of leadership automatically passing on to one of Abbet's sons. Notions of hereditary kingship as was practised by humans, dwarfs and elves was never accepted by the halflings.

Even before Bron Abbet's death, the communities outside of Yangmere had set up their own system of leadership with mayors and town councils selected by the local families, and sheriffs to keep the peace. It wasn't exactly a democratic system since each family cast a vote rather than each person, but it was still definitely self-government. Abbet wisely consulted with these mayors before making important decisions.

After his death, a new council, called the Assembly, was created with a representative from each village and town. They would meet in Yangmere to discuss issues and vote on them. A Head Councillor was selected from the others to serve a three-year term. As time passed and more communities were established, it became impractical to have a representative from each serve on the Assembly. To solve this problem, each of the five shires created its own Shire Council and sent three representatives to the Assembly. In 2325 the meeting location of the Assembly was moved from Yangmere to the town of Hodenburg which had become the largest town in the Shires due to the volume of trade which had developed with Eowolf, the capital of the League of Rhordia.

This system of government has persisted mostly intact to the present day. It should

be noted, that over the centuries the role of female halflings in government has declined slightly. During their wandering days, the halfling families and clans were ruled by the eldest member, male or female. But once they were permanently settled, families tended to grow in size and the women became more and more involved in running households than in running villages and towns. Although though not officially involved in government, it's often the matriarchs of each sprawling family that get together and make the important decisions for each settlement - while the men bicker and argue in the council chambers. Although it's not overly common, women do also serve in the military and will defend their village just as fiercely as the men ranked up alongside them.

Shire Economics

The chief activity of the Shire halflings is undoubtedly agriculture. The lands seem blessed with perfect growing conditions, a stable climate and predictable, mild seasons. For years, renowned scholars and academics have studied the area and there is frequent speculation that sorcery is involved, for the surrounding areas are not nearly as bountiful. However, even the great arch-mages and professors from the Euhedral Library are at a loss to explain the phenomena.

In fields and valleys awash with golden sunshine grow a bewildering variety of crops including wheat, barley, rye, oats, hops, and a large selection of vegetables, especially potatoes. Orchards and vineyards dripping with fruit are common, with wine and beer being a major export. They are also experts in animal husbandry and large herds of cattle. Flocks of sheep and goats cover those areas better suited for grazing than farming. Shire dairy cattle are renowned and the cheese produced is in great demand. Putting their knowledge of animal rearing to good use, in recent years, the Shire military have started breeding a miniature version of the aralez, a fabulous dog-like creature from the plains, large enough to be ridden comfortably as cavalry for the army.

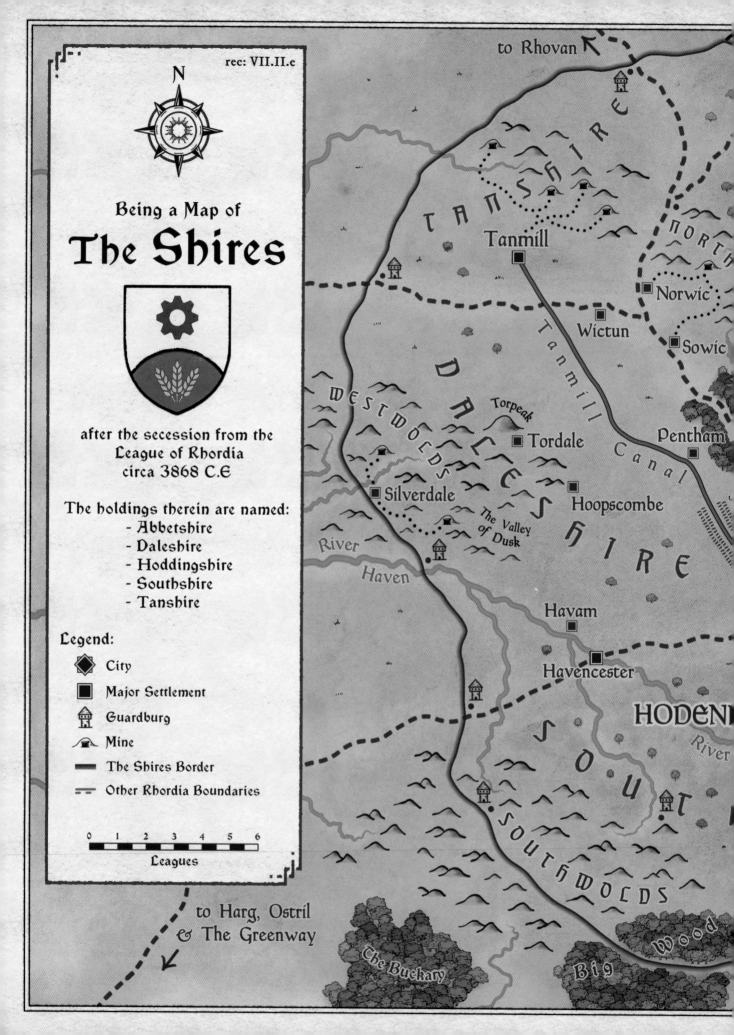

N

rec: VII.II.e

Being a Map of

The Shires

after the secession from the
League of Rhordia
circa 3868 C.E

The holdings therein are named:
- Abbetshire
- Daleshire
- Hoddingshire
- Southshire
- Tanshire

Legend:
- City
- Major Settlement
- Guardburg
- Mine
- The Shires Border
- Other Rhordia Boundaries

0 1 2 3 4 5 6
Leagues

to Harg, Ostril
& The Greenway

to Rhovan

TANSHIRE
NORTH
Tanmill
Norwic
Wictun
Sowic
WESTWOLDS
DALESHIRE
Torpeak
Tordale
Pentham
Silverdale
The Valley
of Dusk
Hoopscombe
River
Haven
Havam
Havencester
HODEN
River
SOUT
SOUTHWOLDS
The Buckary
Big Wood

to Berlonviche

Gennefort

The Forest of Kharne

Ranch expanse

YANGMERE

The Brint

to Torffs Valem

ABBETSHIRE

Abbetsmoor

The Bogs

Aemon's Bluff

Rhordenne

to Hetronburg

The Rhor

The Rhor

EOWOLF

GODDINGSHIRE

Erstford

Erstbridge

Ferchester

Orchards of Huckton

River Erst

Picksbury

Green Glades

River Haven

EASTWOLDS

Golden Fields

Tanmill Canal

to Eowolf

Wolfmoor

The Shires also grow tobacco. The halflings picked up the habit of smoking and the tobacco plants from the dwarfs who are extremely fond of pipe smoking. Once established in the Shires they started growing their own tobacco and have been very successful at it. The local humans are not as avid smokers as dwarfs but there is still a considerable market with them and any excess can be shipped to more distant buyers.

The halflings have put their tinkering skills to good use in supporting their farms and they have ploughs, planters, and reaping machines far superior to those found elsewhere (where they exist at all). This allows the halflings to produce far more food than they need—although halflings actually eat more for their size than humans. The Shires quickly became a significant source of food for the League of Rhordia.

To aid the shipping of Shire goods a system of roads was built connecting the major communities. Although only paved in some areas, they are still well maintained today by the efforts of the community. In later years a canal was constructed between the town of Tanmill and Hodenburg to further help the shipment of freight.

The one thing the Shires are not well-supplied with is metal. There are some mines in the hills around Tanmill, but these have mostly produced copper with lesser amounts of tin and silver. Only a few iron deposits have been found and the quality was generally poor. Iron, therefore has been a major import to the area.

Manufacturing in the Shires occurs mostly in the small workshops that are common in villages, towns, and on individual farms. Only a few places, mostly near Tanmill, produce things on a larger scale. There are just a few foundries in the Shires that can cast iron or bronze in quantity. Obviously, these are very important, but they can only meet local needs. As a result, exports are almost completely limited to foodstuffs and non-metallic handicrafts. Very few metal manufactured goods are exported.

Defending the Shires

From its founding, defence of this new homeland was a major concern for the halflings. No longer able to simply avoid or flee from trouble, they had to be prepared to deal with it head on. The halflings planned for this in two ways: defensive structures and military forces.

Halfling architecture evolved from the simple tents of their wandering days into permanent structures of wood, stone, wattle and daub, and thatch. Initially these were in the same dome shape as the tents, although much larger. They were called cloctans in the halfling tongue. Later, they tended to be eight-sided or twelve-sided in plan because it was easier to build with straight pieces than curved ones, but the upper floors were usually smaller than the lower ones so the same dome or beehive shape of the tents remained. Sometimes dirt would be thrown up to cover walls or roofs and grass grown. The villages and towns tended to be circular in plan, too, reminiscent of the circled wagons used near the end of the wandering days. The halflings never went in for the stone wall defences that humans and others used, but by barricading the spaces between their circled houses they could quickly create a defence when needed. The doors and windows of their houses tended to face the inside of the circle and presented few openings to an attacker coming from outside. As their villages grew into towns, more circular rings were added as needed, but always keeping the potential for defence.

Once the boundaries of the Shires were more or less settled, a series of fortified strongholds called guardburgs were constructed to protect them. These could vary in size from a walled farmhouse or inn with just a dozen people as garrison in more secure areas, to a large post with facilities for several hundred in areas considered dangerous. Patrols would range out from the guardburgs to give advance warning of any approaching threat.

The military forces of the halflings have evolved greatly over time. In their early wandering days every halfling capable of wielding a weapon was expected to be able to fight. Weapons were a variety of spears, axes, and clubs, and of course, bows. Archery had been a favoured halfling pastime from as far back as they can remember. It was a useful skill for gathering food, and in a fight, the ability to strike a (probably larger) foe before they could get close was often the difference between life and death.

Once they became permanently settled, things began to change. With distinct, and generally peaceful borders, fewer and fewer people saw the need for everyone to be ready to fight on a moment's notice. As farmers they had better things to do with their time. Looking at their human neighbours they saw they had people who were full-time soldiers, so the rest could be full time farmers, and the halflings began to adopt similar ways. Not identical, because few halflings wanted to be full-time soldiers, but similar in that some people trained for war, while many more did not.

Each community, or collection of communities, created groups called 'trained bands' to protect them. These were volunteers who spent some of their time drilling, some of their time manning the guardburgs, some of their time patrolling the borders, and some of their time back home doing their normal jobs. They (or more frequently, their families) were paid (usually in food or other goods) for their service. Most of the volunteers were young and unmarried, mostly males, but with a fair number of females, too. As they grew older and started families, they tended to become less active, although many halflings attended at least one training session a year until they reached middle age.

Each Shire had a 'Muster Captain' who inspected and controlled the trained bands in their territory. These were all coordinated by the 'Muster Master', who was the overall commander of the Shires' military. The Muster Master was selected by the Assembly and had a seat in that body.

At first, the trained bands were armed and equipped very simply. Spears were the most common weapons, but there were many archers, too. Archery was a common pastime among the halflings, both for practical purposes, like hunting, but also as a recreation. Archery competitions between the communities were a frequent occurrence and this created a sizeable reserve force in times of crisis in addition to the formal trained bands. The early bands had little in the way of armour beyond simple wooden shields. As more and more ponies were raised, some of the bands became mounted and the Shires fielded light cavalry to better patrol the borders.

With the passage of time the halflings began to see the need for improved equipped and better trained troops. The example of the nearby League of Rhordia and several sharp encounters with roving bands of orcs convinced the Assembly to provide support and funding. First homemade leather armour, and then later metal armour commissioned from the metalsmiths in the League, turned some of the Shires' light infantry into heavy. Some of the largest halflings were given small horses and, clad in metal armour, became their first heavy horse. Both the infantry and cavalry trained in close order movements and formations copied from the humans and after a few years the Shires had a force to be reckoned with. It was well that this was so, because hard times lay ahead.

The War With Winter

In 2499 the so-called War with Winter began. This was another clash of the old gods, the last in modern times. Huge swaths of the world were gripped in a seemingly endless winter that lasted for decades. The halflings—like many of the mortal races—had no idea what brought on this catastrophe, but they were forced to expend every effort to survive. Only their great skill at producing food allowed them pull through. Even so, there was famine and disease and more than half the Shires' population perished. The crisis produced many roving bands of human refugees which had to be turned away by the halflings' trained bands.

Eventually, the war ended and Winter was defeated and the unnatural snows and ice melted with fantastic quickness. Mighty floods followed and the Infant Sea was born, drowning many ancient civilizations. The Shires and the surrounding human kingdoms recovered in time, but the long period of relative peace was over and the Shires were beset with invasions from all manner of foes, both mortal and uncanny, which had been stirred up by the disasters. The reformed trained bands proved up to the challenge, but it was a near-run thing at times.

The Halflings of Ej

Prior to the War with Winter, the Shires were the only permanent halfling settlement in the world. Large numbers of other halflings still roamed the lands, the majority in central Pannithor, hundreds of miles to the south of the Shires. These suffered greatly during the long winter and many more perished in the great flood. Those who survived had to move either north or south to escape the rising waters of the Infant Sea.

Those who went south slowly gathered near the forest of Vieshlar which was in elven territory. The elves, perhaps taking pity on the refugees, welcomed them to their lands and in 3017 a permanent settlement was founded near the elven city of Ej.

The Ej Halflings were more herders than farmers, and living under the protection of their elven hosts, they were able to flourish in their new lands. Retaining their natural affinity for tinkering, and building on the knowledge and skills of the elves, they have developed and produced some wonderous contraptions. Concepts devised for travel and patrolling the mountainous Blades of Ej have developed into fascinating and unique equipment that is slowly finding its way back north, to the military units of the Shires.

Many years after the great floods, the People of Ej made an effort to restore contact with their distant kin from whom they had been sundered by the Infant Sea. In 3255 the people of Hodenburg were astounded to receive a delegation from Ej who had travelled on foot for nearly two years to reach them. Subsequently contact was maintained with a small but steady trickle of people back and forth between the Shires and Ej. Bold young people from both places dared to take The Long Walk as they called it. Activity between the regions has increased significantly in recent years, and old family ties re-established and strengthened. Delegations make bi-annual journeys in both directions, and graceful elven ships now frequently ferry halfling officials and tourists between Lethuia and Valentica, much reducing the length of the journey.

The Rise of the Tinkerers

It took several generations, but eventually a normalcy returned to the Shires after the chaos that followed the end of the long winter. The population rebounded, trade was re-established, and halfling civilization progressed, one mirrored in the nearby League of Rhordia. The League, like the Shires, was a small confederation surrounded by many potential enemies. They could not hope to match all their foes by raw strength, so they did so by being smarter. The League became a centre of learning with an emphasis on science, engineering, and to a lesser extent, the magical arts. For better defence they established the College of Warcraft in Eowolf, one of the only institutions of its kind anywhere. Their halfling neighbours soon saw the benefits in this and many of their best tinkerers migrated to the League cities to learn.

And learn they did. In an amazingly short time the sophistication of halfling tinkering advanced dramatically. Farm implements became even more efficient and the halflings were soon constructing windmills to grind their grain and farm yields became so great that they began construction of the canal from Tanmill to Hodenburg to better move them. The canal was a huge undertaking in resources and manpower and took over ten years to complete, but once finished was a local wonder.

Advances were made in military equipment as well. The League had begun to adopt crude gun powder weapons by copying the techniques of the dwarfs and the halflings quickly followed suit. They still preferred bows over muskets, but they were soon casting their own cannons and a small gunpowder mill was built in Tanmill.

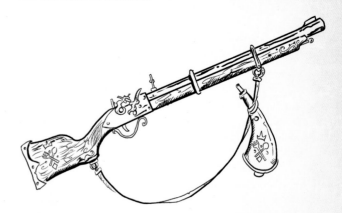

Some of the halflings advanced far beyond the tinkering stage and became engineers and even artificers capable of creating items imbued with magic. A few became legendary figures in the Shires. Percival Arbuckle and later his apprentice Paddy Bobart made great advances in the creation of artillery and both made copies of the dwarf Steel Behemoth war machines. Bobart, in his later years, founded an engineering and magical research centre in the hills north of Tanmill based on the League's College of Warcraft.

Magic users had always been a rarity among halflings. While some of them, like Arbuckle and Bobart had limited abilities and could use magic in the devices they created, very few had the abilities of the classic wizards. Those that did were highly prized, by the Assembly and Muster Master, but it was rare to have more than one or two at a time. Even so, the halflings were always finding new ways to use even their modest skills. A prime example is the recently revealed innovation of imbuing food with magic. Alchemists had known how to make magical potions for millennia, but these were usually only a single draught affecting a single person. The halfling 'Gastromancy' as it has been dubbed can create a magical effect that can be served to hundreds or even thousands at a time. One of the first widely known practitioners is a halfling woman named Mama Beata and she has gone on to teach others her art. Thus halfling armies often have rations which can extend endurance, increase strength, and give courage.

Joining the League of Rhordia

As the centuries passed, the Shires and the League of Rhordia grew closer and closer. Trade between them became a vital part of both economies. The League was especially dependent on Shires-grown food, and the halflings got most of their metals from the League. More than a few halflings moved to the human cities of the League to expand their businesses and a few humans even relocated to the Shires. The trade became so important that the Tanmill Canal was extended all the way to the League city of Eowulf.

Military cooperation was established and threats to their borders were often met by joint halfling-human armies. In 3712 a particularly dangerous orc invasion was defeated by the combined armies and ten years later the Shires formally joined the League.

It was a mutually beneficial arrangement, but not without some drawbacks. The League became more and more dependent on food imports from the Shires and the Shires became more and more dependent on the military power of the League to defend it. The halflings, never natural soldiers, slowly let their heavy infantry and cavalry units dwindle, fielding more and more light infantry and cavalry, such as they had in the early days of the trained bands. As long as the alliance with the League remained strong, this wasn't a serious problem and, in fact, the combination of League heavy infantry and cavalry teamed with the light cavalry and infantry of the Shires proved a very effective one.

But sadly the alliance with the League collapsed with shocking swiftness.

The Broken Alliance

About a century after the forming of the alliance, relations between the Shires and the League started to deteriorate. The humans accused the halflings of overcharging on the food they sold them, and the halflings complained that the taxes they paid to support the League military were too high. Insidious, anti-halfling feelings and aggressive non-human policies began circulating and infecting the League. Many cast suspicious eyes at the mysterious and sinister advisors that had slowly begun to appear at the sides of the League barons. Other rumours linked the change in opinion to the same wave of human-centric politics emanating from Valentica and spreading north. At first it was just grumbling, but soon it became more serious with anti-halfling violence in the League cities growing at an alarming rate. A few suspected that this crumbling of friendship had some darker source, but could not discover it.

After only a few years things became so serious that the Shires withdrew from the League, and established a trade embargo against them. The League, fearing a famine without Shire-grown food, declared war and began a campaign to subjugate the Shires and turn them into serfs.

The initial battles went badly for the halflings and they realised that allowing their heavy infantry and cavalry to disappear had been a serious mistake. They were routed at a battle south of Hodenburg and the capital and several other towns were put under siege.

Had it not been for the foresight of Paddy Bobart the war surely would have been lost. He had established his centre for science and engineering in a secret place called the Holdfast north of Tanmill and was assembling a new army, much better equipped than the other halfling forces. By good fortune, shortly before the war broke out a delegation from the Ej Halflings had arrived, not on foot but in a wonderous flying machine. They brought other amazing devices and pledged their help in the coming conflict.

By even greater fortune, the Shires had among them a military commander of outstanding talent. Aeron Cadwallader had been a cadet at the League's College of Warcraft, but returned home when the Shires left the League. Although young, he quickly proved his worth and Bobart placed him in command of the new army.

Aided by the Ej Halflings, Mama Beata's magic food, and every mage the Shires could muster, Cadwallader began a lightning campaign that routed the League forces at the Battle of Picksbury and then raised the siege of Hodenburg and sent the League forces reeling back into their own territory.

The war between the Shires and the League came to a sudden end when it was realised that they had all been betrayed. The dispute between them had been deliberately created by foreign spies working for Lord Darvled, a tyrant from south of the Dragon Teeth Mountains. It had all been a plot to disrupt the League and prepare it for an invasion by a large mercenary army. Eowolf was placed under siege and it appeared the League was doomed to be conquered.

Despite many misgivings, the Shires put aside their differences and came to the aid of the League. Cadwallader again devised a daring plan and the mercenaries were defeated and scattered and the League saved.

The Present Day

Politically, both the Shires and the settlements in Ej remain mostly neutral, only getting involved in affairs that directly affect, or benefit them. This attitude is common amongst individuals too. They are kind and pleasant, generous too at times, but equally prepared to let others sort out their own problems and remain aloof.

Although the differences between the Shires and the League of Rhordia have been patched up and pledges of friendship made, the Shires have not re-joined the League and do not intend to. Nor have they forgotten the lessons they learned. They now maintain a well-balanced and well-led army of their own. While they will cooperate with the League when it suits them, the Shires' defence is in the hands of the halflings alone.

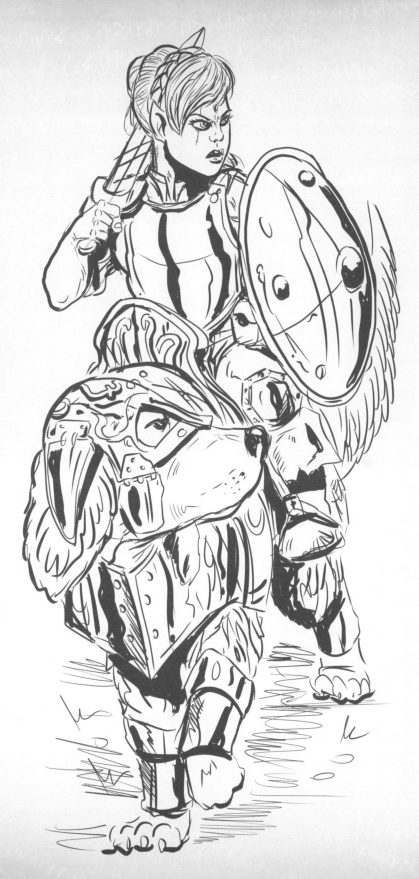

RIFTFORGED ORCS

From deep within the Abyss, the Wicked One Garkan the Black has toiled for millennia at his soul forges. Always seeking new ways to unleash terror upon the unsuspecting world, it seemed even for Garkan that he would never better his warlike creations, the orcs. Until now...

When the Abyssal Dwarfs inadvertently unleashed the Nexus of Power beneath the Halpi Mountains, the surge of magical energy was felt across all of Pannithor – a violent tear in the very fabric of reality, sufficient to distort even the Elven Ways, and widen the Abyss. Though 'Halpi's Rift', as it became known, was eventually capped by an alliance of the noble races, it was not before the Nexus had wreaked considerable destruction upon the world and its terrible power felt from pole to pole.

At the height of the Nexus' surge of energy, before the forces of good pushed back the armies of evil, there came a moment when the Southern Rift and the Abyss were infused with such power that the veil tore entirely, and the two pits of darkness were linked as one beneath Pannithor. At such an unholy coupling, Oskan himself saw that the time had come to herald in a new age of darkness. Oskan summoned Garkan, and together they formulated a plan to destroy all that was good in the world. Garkan harnessed the power of the violent, unnatural storms that raged across the world above, the flesh forges of the Fourth Circle came alive with energy hitherto unseen, and the souls of the tormented cried out in anguish. At this sign, Garkan the Black summoned his underlings, and set about the forges with renewed vigour. As the battle for Halpi's rift raged in the mortal realm, Garkan selected the prime cuts from the fallen to fuel his twisted experiments. The orcs had always been his greatest accomplishment, but now, with this new power in his hands, Garkan strove to improve on his dark design.

Children of Garkan

Their twisted bodies animated by the power of a raging storm, their souls infused with very essence of the Nexus, the orcs that emerged from Garkan's flesh forges were unlike any that had come before them. Their cracked skin was of a green-grey hue, and broader, more muscular, and yet possessed of a cruel cunning and impressive martial prowess, these 'Riftforged orcs' were truly Garkan's finest creation.

But there was more to these creatures than mere brute strength. Their affinity with the rift-storms brought about by the Nexus of Power manifested in crackling energy, which wreathed their bodies and lent strength to their sword-arms. The more Riftforged orcs gathered, the greater this power became, and with extraordinary swiftness the young race

began to master this energy, fuelling it with their battle-rage. The greatest among them could command the elements, blackening the skies and bringing storms wherever they trod. These, Garkan called Stormbringers, the commanders of the new horde. But the Stormbringers were possessed of tempers quick as the lightning they commanded, and few would suffers others to live. Their competitive nature and martial pride was untameable, and many died in the early days of their creation, challenging each other to duels that shook the very halls of the Abyss. They fought not only for power and position, but also to win the favour of Garkan. For unlike the lesser orcs that had come before, the Riftforged orcs recognised their creator, and swore unshakeable fealty to him. Garkan the Black was pleased. With an army of these creatures, his own status amongst the Wicked Ones would surely grow. But he would not share this power – the Riftforged orcs were his to command, for one day Garkan the Black might have need of them to wage war on his brother gods. The Riftforged orcs pay lip-service to Oskan, Talus and Barglurath, but their true allegiance is never in question. One thing they share with all Wicked Ones, however, is a deep and burning hatred of the Shining Ones and all they stand for. The Riftforged orcs would wipe out everything that is good and pure in the world if they could have their way.

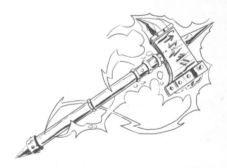

For a year and a day, Garkan toiled at his forges, expanding the ranks of the Riftforged orcs, creating legions of heavily armoured warriors, all under the command of the warmongering Stormbringers. Lesser demons whipped shackled souls to work ceaselessly, forging weapons and armour for Garkan's new horde. Each brutish warrior would go into battle protected by thick armour plates, carved with the likenesses of leering Abyssals, and crackling with coruscating energy. With their great strength, they wield heavy hammers and carry thick shields, often jagged and spiked with lightning devices. The march of their mail-shod feet shakes the ground like the thunder they summon, and though they are more adept at strategy and battle-tactics than any orc before them, their battle-fury is wild as the untamed storms.

War in the Abyss

The Abyss itself proved the most effective testing ground for these new warriors. Gibbering demons provoked Garkan's new creations to battle almost at once, seeing them as mortal interlopers in their realm. Garkan granted the Stormbringers permission to seek retribution as they saw fit, and so the Riftforged orcs marched to war. Over myriad campaigns spanning many years, the Riftforged orcs fought battle after battle in Garkan's name, hunting in the second circle, braving the fires of the fourth circle, enduring the tortures of the third circle, and battling the champions of the fifth circle. In the Abyss, death is not the end, and so the orc warriors fought, and fell, and rose to fight again, each resurrection making them stronger, cannier, and more skilled. In those campaigns, veterans emerged from the ranks, along with great leaders and shamanic Stormcallers.

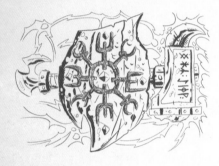

So powerful did the Riftforged legions become that their arrogance grew to match their strength. They came to despise weakness of any kind, looking down upon the races of the world, even the lesser forces of the Abyss. The weak within their own ranks are routinely culled, and the leaders of their forces control the horde only while they can rule with an iron hand – should they falter, they will quickly be deposed. However, such ruthlessness leads to discipline: every Riftforged orc follows orders without question, for they know their commanders rose to prominence through strength and determination alone. They earned their authority, and for as long as they bring glorious victories for their legion, their word is law. From amongst the most cunning and tactically minded Stormbringers, Garkan selected his most trusted lieutenants, naming them the Storm Marshalls. In effect a Riftforged Council, the Storm Marshalls have the authority to bring entire legions to heel in Garkan's name, and are powerful enough to command the respect of a dozen or more Stormbringers.

Over long campaigns, the Riftforged legions became well-organised, autonomous fighting forces, each with their own heraldry, traditions, and favoured strategies. The banners of legions such as the Drakeslayers, Thunderborn, and Blackhammers, quickly became legend within the Abyss, putting flight to hordes of Diaboli through sheer dread reputation. It was then that Garkan looked upon what he had wrought, and knew the time had come. The Riftforged

orcs had been born unto lightning, tempered in the fires of the Abyss, and now had but one more challenge to face. They would be unleashed into the mortal world, and carve their own path of glory and destruction in Garkan's name. It was time to set them free.

Legions Unbound

Time does not flow as expected within the Abyss. The Riftforged orcs had campaigned through Abyssal circles for well over a decade, yet when they emerged into the world of mortals barely a year had passed since the capping of Halpi's Rift. Legion after legion poured from the Abyss with grim purpose, marching tirelessly to the drum-like rumble of thunder. The Stormbringers had been given full autonomy by Garkan – they would march upon the lands of men, Elves, and Dwarfs. They would show the servants of the thrice-cursed Shining Ones the true meaning of power.

The fickle powers of the Abyss had split the hordes across half the world. Some legions poured into Tragar, where the Abyssal Dwarfs had been forewarned to stand aside, and advanced upon the Halpi Mountains, drawn to the site of the now-closed Rift that had led to their creation. Others ventured into Barica, while most went west across the Mammoth Steppe, battling ogre tribes in their first real test of strength. Most of these legions continued west across the Ardovikian Plain, where at last they found their most determined foes in the race of men. Advancing into the League of Rhordia, three full legions began a systematic invasion of those lands, sacking and razing every settlement in their path. Other legions, unable to cooperate with their arrogant kin for long, went instead to Basilea, where they assaulted the Brothermark in the most violent incursion the Basileans had seen in over a century. Two fortresses of the Brotherhood Watchline have so far fallen, and the orcs have proven impossible to evict. Farthest north, the Riftforged orcs struck out across the Frozen Sea. Fighting both the hostile environment and the hardy Varangur, these legions slowly dwindled in size. And yet rumour has it that they have taken a foothold in the Ice Mountains, where they yet gather their strength.

Meanwhile, south of Ophidia, great storms raged, heralding the arrival of the Riftforged orcs at the mouth of the Southern Rift. The march of the legions, as always, was heralded by gathering thunderclouds. Torrents of lashing rain fell upon the Cracked Lands for the first time in many years, flashes of lightning illuminated thousands of heavily armoured orcs, ready for conquest in a strange land. Most began the long march across the Windblown Basin, determined to seek out the Elves so hated by their master, Garkan. They have already navigated the southern jungles, their glowing eyes fixed on Ej and Elvenholme. Some even ventured east to the Empire of Dust, but these have not been heard of since.

War for Orc-Kind

Wherever the Riftforged orcs have fought, they have found other, lesser orcs, who they see as Garkan's failed experiments. Sometimes, tribes of these lesser orcs refuse to be subjugated by their larger cousins, and instead resist with all their might. On some very few occasions, orc tribes of sufficient size and power have succeeded in driving off the predations of the Riftforged orcs - but these feats are few and far between. For the most part, when the Riftforged orcs encounter an orc tribe, the lesser orcs are either defeated in short order, or immediately recognise the superior strength of their strange new kin, and join with them willingly for the chance of greater glory on the field of battle.

For the Riftforged orcs, Youngax tribes make the perfect foot-soldiers. They are keen to fight, almost numberless, and yet are highly unlikely to ever challenge the hierarchy of the legion. These aspirants wish to join the vaunted ranks of the legion, hoping to be recognised for singular acts of barbarism or bloodshed by their betters. Should they fall in battle, they are sent to Garkan's forges, where - if they survive the process - they may be reborn as a Riftforged warrior. In this way, the legion can always replenish its numbers, while the Youngax followers look on in awe as their former kin seemingly returns from the grave in a powerful new form. For the Youngax, there could be no greater ambition than to achieve such power. For the new Riftforged warrior, however, their former life is but the ghost of a dream; their entire will now focused upon serving their legion, for the greater glory of Garkan.

A Storm In The Shires

A Storm Unleashed

Heralded by blackening skies and pealing thunder, the Riftforged Legions emerged from the Abyss with nought but conquest on their minds. Hordes of regimented orcs, battle skills honed by years of campaigning in the Abyssal realm, set their sights on the servants of the Shining Ones, determined to wreak destruction in the name of Garkan.

The Legions, seemingly autonomous fighting forces, marched in all directions. They fought the Varangur upon the ice floes of the Frozen Sea; they razed fishing villages to the ground all along the coast of Carrog; they battled dwarfs on the mountain slopes of Abercarr; they besieged the watchlines of the Brothermark. The rampage of the Riftforged orcs was brutal and far-reaching.

Where the advance of the Riftforged Legions passed through the territory of common orc tribes, something extraordinary happened that would be of utmost concern to all civilised peoples. The orcs, so impressed by the intellect, strength, and strange powers of the heavily armoured legions, joined forces with them, turning the legions into vast hordes. Certainly, some Krudgers of sufficient infamy and strength resisted the rule of their strange, storm-calling kin, but these Krudgers were few and far between. Most were subjugated, or willingly gave their entire tribe over to the legions. And so, those Riftforged Legions that had marched west across the Mammoth Steppe, and as far as the Ardovikian Plain, grew in such numbers as to turn their measured advance into an avalanche of destruction.

The Torffs Valem Massacre

It was upon the Fields of Arbrin, an hour's ride north of Torffs Valem, that the legions first made their presence known in Rhordia, and there recorded their most devastating and infamous victory. At that time, Torffs Valem had been plagued by a great orc horde, led by a grizzled Krudger known as Krakok One-Eye. The army of Torffs Valem had mustered against the horde, and ridden out across the valley, where they met the orcs in battle. Though the orcs were great in number, the men of Rhordia drove their cavalry into the heart of the orc force, and there rode down Krakok One-Eye and his personal bodyguard of Morax warriors. Sent into disarray, the orcs fled, following the River Brint northwards, pursued every step of the way by the jubilant members of the League.

When at last they reached the Fields of Arbrin – a flat, open plain stretching beneath the wooded hills of Armbul – the League checked its advance. The orcs had ceased their flight,

and now amassed once more into fighting ranks. Overhead, the skies blackened, and the heavens opened. The League wizards sensed danger ahead, and counselled the captains to withdraw from the field, but the proud warriors of Torffs Valem would not hear of it. They formed their lines, and prepared for open battle. Lightning streaked across a slate grey sky, illuminating another force amassing behind Krakok's tribe. Countless orcs had come as if from nowhere, heavily armoured, ranks in meticulous order, eyes glowing with the very power of the storm. They advanced in unison through the driving rain, mail-shod boots shaking the ground.

Trusting to the tactics that had seen off countless orc invaders, the Rhordians marshalled their cavalry and charged en masse – but this time they charged to their doom. The common orcs threw themselves recklessly into battle, seemingly to impress the newcomers as to their bravery. By the time the armoured lines of the legion was met, the knights of the League were already faltering. The leaders of the orc legion, lightning crackling around their hulking forms, bellowed commands at their warriors, and the Riftforged orcs counter-charged with the unstoppable force of a raging storm. It was a massacre.

By sunset, almost every warrior of the League was slain or fleeing, the blood of the fallen washing down to the river. Before the next dawn the legion had reached the gates of Torffs Valem. By midday the city walls were burning, and the Riftforged were already marching south. Their cruel work done.

The League Beset

The Riftforged legion, which became known as the Abyssal Eyes due to the baleful heraldry of their banners, marched upon village after village, outpost after outpost, leaving a trail of burning farmsteads and shattered militia posts in their wake. Twice, the Dukes of Rhordia sought to meet the Abyssal Eyes in battle, and twice they were put to flight – although their valiant efforts at least slowed the legion's advance. This gave the League the opportunity to muster a grand army, uniting provinces under the command of Duke Hetronburg and Baron Gennefort. Under lashing rain and crackling lightning, the two armies met in bitter battle that raged a day and a night. When Gennefort's own knights launched a devastating charge, it seemed that at last the tide had turned. The storm eased for just a moment, the Abyssal Eyes faltered.

And then, presaged by a crack of lightning that gouged the very earth, a second army crested the hill. The booming war-chants of a new Riftforged Legion carried on the howling winds, and Duke Hetronburg knew all was lost.

The Abyssal Eyes, under the leadership of their Stormbringer, Grullik Headpuller, had known great success on the campaign trail, but their numbers were dwindling. Reluctantly, Grullik was forced to acknowledge the newcomer, Zargok, of the Blackhammer Legion, as commander-in-chief of the campaign. Their tenuous alliance was sufficient to bring Gennefort to its knees, before the horde marched upon the walled town of Rhordenne, sacking it after a five-day siege. This event marked a turning point in Rhordia's history – armies mustered across the League and beyond as word of the invasion spread. Zargok, determining that besting the humans was the more glorious path, took most of his legion east to face the Lords of Rhordia. With a few cohorts of Blackhammer legionaries as reinforcements, along with the bulk of the Youngax rabble who had tagged along for the fight, Grullik's Abyssal Eyes marched on, to see what lay beyond the Rhordian borders.

A Shattered Peace

Meanwhile, in the peaceful Shires, word of the sacking of Rhordenne had arrived to mixed reception. Many halflings disbelieved that mere orcs could bring such a well defended town so low, blaming the news on the notoriously exaggerated tales of wandering human bards. However, the halfling elders were swayed to action by Aeron Cadwallader, the Shires' greatest hero and youngest halfling to hold the rank of Muster-Master. Cadwallader's most trusted scouts had seen for themselves the strange nature of these new orcs, and so a council of the greatest commanders of the Shire was convened. Cadwallader convinced the Elders that the orcs were coming, whether some chose to believe it or not. Worse, there would be no help from outside – the League of Rhordia was beset by its own invasion, and assisting

in any kind of defence of the Shires would be the last thing on their minds.

By piecing together fragmented tales of these so-called 'Riftforged orcs', the halflings formulated a strategy of sorts. It was Dilwyn Brynmoor, Chief Artificer of the Shires, who came up with the theory that the march of the orcs was akin to the path of a fierce lightning storm, and like lightning it could be forked – split multiple times so its power would dissipate. The men of Rhordia had failed, Brynmoor said, because they'd allowed the orcs to dictate the time and place of battle, and thus Rhordenne had been sundered like a tree struck by a lightning bolt.

Studying their maps, the halflings determined that the Abyssal Eyes would come from the north and east, following the road from Rhordenne. They formed a twofold plan to halt the orcs' advance. A scouting force was sent north-east via the forest trails to pull as many orcs as possible away from the main column of march, while a larger militia force went north to the crossings on the river Erst. There, they would destroy the Erstbridge, forcing the orcs to ford the river, where they would be met by bow and spear. Even Cadwallader was not confident of victory against so mighty a foe, but the people of the Shires, peaceful as they were, were no cowards. The militia would divert the orcs from the most populated towns, and fight to the last.

Battle is Joined

The scouting force passed through the Forest of Kharne, and finally caught up with the Riftforged column less than half a league from Erstford. At once, they set about plaguing the orcs until at last the legion could ignore them no longer. Three full cohorts turned from the main column, marching inexorably under the barrage of archery. The halflings retreated in good order whence they had come, leading the legionaries as far as The Bogs. Realising their mistake too late, the orc cohorts became mired in the treacherous terrain, and were ill-prepared for the halflings' trap – an army of Abbetshire emerged from the forests, assailing the orcs from all sides. When at last the orcs fought their way to open ground, they were met by aralez cavalry and the debilitating magic of halfling Saucerors. The legionary commanders fought bravely, but without support they floundered in the face of a swift enemy on home territory, and by a thousand cuts they succumbed to the halfling attack. A few scattered remnants of the legionary force fled into the Northwolds, where they were forced to battle the hill-folk in a series of bitter skirmishes.

Meanwhile, at Erstford, things did not go quite as planned. The Riftforged had reached the destroyed Erstbridge, but like a force of nature had not diverted to the ford where the halfling army waited. Instead, with grim efficiency they set about hacking through the nearby woodland. Hulking, ogre-like monstrosities lent their strength to the effort, and soon the orcs had created a pair of huge floating bridges, wide enough for their cohorts to march across. Such ingenuity and organisation had never before been seen from orc-kind, and the halflings barely had time to redeploy before the legion had reached the south bank of the Erst. When battle was joined, it was with a ferocity that the halflings had not expected. Lightning flashed across the sky, hulking Ambarox seared the halfling ranks with blasts of coruscating energy, and then the legion advanced, protected by thick armour, crushing all who dared stand before them.

Led by Conwy Macsen, a commander renowned for quick-thinking and flexible strategy, the halflings quickly reorganised. They had got the orcs' attention, and now Macsen's job was to lead the enemy away from the towns of the Shires. If the Riftforged were a thunderstorm, then Macsen needed a lightning rod to redirect their strength – and that rod was the long line of border towers that stood watch over the eastern boundaries.

Messengers were sent ahead on swift aralez to warn of the coming danger. Some were slain as they tried to flee the battle by vicious Helstrike Manticores, and were it not for the intervention of a small squadron of Ej Grenadiers, none would have escaped. Having done all he could, Macsen ordered his forces to scatter, with the bulk forming a fighting retreat to the south, the legion harrying them every step of the way. The rest of the force stole away to Hodenburg, with Macsen's hastily-written contingency plan.

In the days that followed, the border towers fell one-by-one. At each tower, the militia assembled, fought, but fled before the casualties mounted. The towers were blasted with lightning and razed to the ground. Each time, the halflings retreated towards the next tower. And yet unbeknownst to the orcs, a portion of each force later scattered, disappearing into the hills and forests, and making their way to Hodenburg. This was Macsen's gambit – the Shirefolk would conceal their true strength, and instead gather the greatest

army the Shires had ever seen at their capital. Macsen prayed it would not be needed – as much as he had faith in the people, the Riftforged orcs were like nothing he'd ever seen before. He would rather they did not set foot within a hundred leagues of the fair city of Hodenburg.

When the twin watchtowers of Tanmill fell, the exhausted Macsen knew he could do no more. The orcs of the Abyssal Eye had discovered the Tanmill Canal, and immediately recognised its strategic importance. No amount of goading by the ragtag halfling militia could now keep them from their prize – Grullik Headpuller organised his remaining legion and followed the canal north, into the heartlands of the Shires.

The Battle of Green Glades

From the steady stream of Macsen's battlefield reports, the council at Hodenburg had plotted the orcs' path around the Shires' border. The legion had dwindled somewhat in size, but was still too powerful to fight in open war – the walls of Hodenburg could not hold against a foe that could command the very elements. When messages reached them that the orcs had turned towards the city, Aeron Cadwallader sent word to the Feastmasters of the Green Glades to delay the orcs while the city prepared its defences.

So it was that when the skies above the Golden Fields blackened, and the orcs approached the great forest of Green Glades, the trees came alive with the exuberant hollering of halfling gangs. The Feastmasters of the glades were possessed of extraordinary knowledge of woodcraft and archery, and they turned all of their skills against the invaders. Finally, the orcs were forced to abandon their staunch battle tactics, their shield walls proving more a hindrance than a help against an enemy that hid in the forest paths. In skirmish bands, the orcs finally seemed beatable. Only the hulking Thunderseers were able to match the halflings in woodland, their gifts of foresight and keen senses uniting as they hunted the braves on their own territory. However, their numbers were few, and the rest of the cohorts suffered terribly.

Grullik, realising too late there was more to these small folk than met the eye, signalled for the cohorts to fall back to the meadows. To cover their retreat, he roared orders to the hordes of Youngax who had followed him all the way from the Ardovikian Plain. At his command, the Youngax charged headlong into the woods, dying in droves to halfling arrows, but covering the retreat of the legionaries. Those Youngax who finally got to grips with the braves set about the fight with unbridled ferocity, for to prove themselves in the eyes of the Headpuller – and to Garkan – was the greatest ambition they could imagine.

His losses already unacceptable, Grullik marched what was left of the legion around the outskirts of the forest, staying as far from the range of the halfling bows as he could, abandoning the Youngax to the war effort. If they wiped out the halflings, so much the better, but at the very least they would keep them busy for days to come.

The Defence of Hodenburg

To the rumble of thunder and the lashing of rain, the Riftforged orcs assaulted the walls of Hodenburg. Wave after wave drove against the city walls, while the defences were blasted with elemental power, and a gargantuan Storm Giant pounded at the gates. Watching from the tallest tower, Aeron Cadwallader turned to Dilwyn Brynmoor once more – the artificer whose theories had proven accurate before – and posited an unorthodox strategy.

The orcs were no patient siege-masters, as their hasty attack on Torffs Valem had shown. They assaulted the walls ceaselessly, again and again, drawing power from the fighting, while their leaders crackled with elemental energy. It seemed that the more the orcs fought, the more angry the storm grew, and the more punishing their assault. If the Riftforged Legion could indeed be likened to a thunderbolt, then the halflings would once more have to split its power, forking the lightning into less destructive fragments. Reluctantly, the Elders agreed to Cadwallader's plans. Preparations were made across the city. And then, in an act that some considered reckless, but others prayed was genius, Cadwallader opened the gates.

The Abyssal Eyes ploughed through the gates, flooding into the city square. They met little resistance, but instead found many of the streets inaccessible, barricaded at Cadwallader's orders. Fully one third of the legion rushed through the northern streets, before the barricades were closed behind them. Another third was funnelled around the inner walls, down the slopes that led to the Grainbarn beneath the city, and again the way behind was shut. The remainder, including Grullik himself, were trapped in the courtyard, where finally the halflings mustered for battle.

The Battle of the Great Heath

The orcs that ravaged north found themselves shepherded to the Great Heath – a vast public 'garden' resembling a hilly meadow set about with lush wooded groves, characteristic of the orchards favoured by the halflings. Helstrikers took to the skies to scout a way of the seemingly deserted heath, only to discover a strange-looking halfling army speeding towards the orc lines.

This was like nothing the Riftforged had encountered before. Blackpowder carbines roared in armour-piercing volleys, while Ej Grenadiers, on secondment to the Shires, darted past the Helstrikers and dropped their explosive charges into the orc lines, disrupting the legionaries' ranks. Before the orcs could recover from the onslaught, the air was filled by the sounds of clanking and whirring. From the gunsmoke rolled troll-powered Harvesters, blades whirring and churning, scything through the Riftforged ranks with abandon. The Helstrikers turned back to assist the ground forces, only to find themselves peppered with shot by Aeronauts, who had drifted gracefully over the Great Heath in their balloons. Helpless to intervene, the Helstrikers could only watch as the halflings smashed into the legionaries' lines with Aralez cavalry and monstrous Iron Beasts. Only then did the bugles sound, and the halfling Spearspikes advanced

over the hills, led by Conwy Macsen who was now eager for revenge. The Spearspikes hunted the stragglers and wounded with venomous spite, while the Harvesters ploughed ahead, watering the meadow with orc blood.

Over the heath, the rain lightened, and a shaft of sunlight peeked through the clouds. The storm weakened, as Cadwallader had predicted. The orcs were put to flight, and with one last rueful look over their shoulders, the Helstrikers flew from the city lest they meet the same end as their fellows.

The Raid on the Grainbarn

Those orcs who had ventured underground were at first confident. After all what, was a mere dark dungeon to the endless cavernous horrors of the Abyss? And indeed, what they now found themselves within was a dungeon – the Grainbarn, a vast underground storehouse supplying food and beer to all the public buildings of Hodenburg. Many of the orcs could not resist helping themselves to kegs of delicious ale, and while they drank, they were unaware of movement in the long shadows...

The Grainbarn is a sprawling storehouse also for many rare and exotic – and, some whisper, forbidden – ingredients.

Thus, it is the domain of the Saucerors, and foremost among them, Mama Beata. There, in the darkness, Mama Beata had marshalled her gastromancers, passing enchanted rations around the troops at her disposal to imbue them with strength and courage belying their diminutive size. But she planned not on meeting the orcs with braves alone.

The Riftforged orcs were alerted to the presence of halflings by their Stormslayers – these brutish creatures scented the enemy, and began lumbering towards the hidden braves. When they were close enough that the halflings could see their glowing eyes, Mama Beata gave the order. Cages were opened, and the long-kept secret of the Saucerors was unleashed. Greedyguts – brutish, mutated halfling warriors bloated and empowered by gastromantic feasts – now lurched from the dark. The sounds of ferocious battle between Stormslayers and Greedyguts echoed through the Larder. The orcs ceased their revelry and formed into their cohorts, but the halflings had used the darkness to their advantage. They struck from hidden tunnels, fired volleys of arrows from walkways, while gun-dogs sniped the orc leaders from concealed niches and culverts. Saucerors assailed the foe with their magic and explosive potions, and when the cohorts were forced to scatter, the halflings took up the hunt, whooping and hollering through the echoing tunnels, hunting orcs in the dungeons, until they were nought but food for the insatiable Greedyguts.

The Fight for Hodenburg Square

The fiercest fighting took place in the great square behind the city gates. Here, the Riftforged were encircled by halfling braves on all sides, led by Aeron Cadwallader himself. But the orcs included Grullik and his personal guard, not to mention the bulk of the legion's support troops. The Storm Giant lumbered forward, setting about the barricades, plucking gun-dogs from their elevated positions on balconies and devouring them. Stormcallers blasted ranks of Spearspikes with powerful lightning bolts. Thunderseers avoided halfling volleys unerringly, their prescience guiding them into combat where their brutish strength could tear the smallfolk asunder.

And yet here the halflings had numbers on their side. They had the pride - nay, the very survival - of all the Shires at stake. If the orcs had previously seen only a diminutive people, rustic and slow to anger, he now saw a spiteful, vicious race of tiny warriors, each willing to sell their lives dearly to defend their city. Gunfire cracked from every window. Strange sorcery beset the orcs, filling the square with debilitating fumes. As the battle raged, a squadron of balloons drifted overhead, their aeronauts dropping grenades into the orc ranks. With their arrival came the news that the Battle for the Great Heath was won. The halflings took heart from the news, redoubling their efforts, closing their net on the surrounded orcs.

Grullik called for the Stormslayers to charge the halflings, but the order could not be carried out. Behind the orcs, through the city gates, came a roar of bestial rage. Forest trolls, goaded northwards by the enraged Feastmasters of the Green Glades, now launched their own charge. Troll and Stormslayer met in an earth-shaking clash of violence.

When the surviving Greedyguts emerged from the Grainbarn, it became apparent that the battle for the underground had also been won. They made for the Storm Giant, sensing a wondrous feast. They leapt upon the behemoth, dragging it to the ground, and though half their number perished in the attempt, they brought the giant low. Grullik saw his legion in tatters, his closest cohorts all that remained, battling pint-sized soldiers that should barely be able to pick up a spear, let alone slay one of his mighty legionaries with it. And then from the halfling ranks came Aeron Cadwallader himself, barging through the orc line on an aralez, leaping from his mount into single combat with Grullik. Massive axe met enchanted blade. Lightning crackled around Grullik, but slowly fizzled out, the power of the storm abating with each fallen legionary. Cadwallader was relentless, spinning and slashing, a whirling ball of fury.

Sensing defeat, Grullik called to his bodyguard. They closed ranks, forcing Cadwallader away. Orc drums beat out the command to fall back, while Grullik Headpuller, and the remnants of his legion, fled the city, peppered all the way by the arrows of the Green Glades reinforcements. At last, the clouds fully parted, and the sun shone upon the city of Hodenburg.

What Price Victory?

What became of Grullik Headpuller, who could tell? His shattered legion would be hunted across the Shires and beyond for weeks and months to come. Cadwallader's victory was one of the greatest ever recorded in the Shires, and cemented his fame as the halflings' greatest ever commander. But the cost of the victory weighed heavily upon Cadwallader's brow. Had he been more decisive when word had first reached them, perhaps they could have inflicted heavier casualties on the orcs at Erstford - perhaps they could have even stopped them altogether. Then the guardburgs would not have burned - a devastation that would take much time to undo. And though the songs of Hodenburg's defence told of glory and heroism, they failed to account for the true cost. How many braves had fallen? How many citizens?

Aeron Cadwallader had indeed met the sternest test in the Shires' modern history, but he knew the Abyssal Eyes were but one legion of Riftforged orcs. If they could cause such destruction, what would happen should they return, and in greater numbers? He prayed he would never have to find out...

A Storm In The Shires Campaign

Playing the Campaign

This campaign is designed to allow you and a friend to play through the narrative of the Riftforged Orcs' invasion of the Halfling Shines. However it is also easy to substitute either, or both, armies for forces in your existing collections and to set the campaign in whatever location you wish to tell a story.

Each scenario depicts a different stage of the invasion, however it is entirely possible that your games will provide different results than those detailed in the official narrative!

From scenario two onwards, each scenario will detail which player is the Attacker and which is the Defender, and this will be determined by the result of a previous encounter.

There are four narrative campaign scenarios, followed by a three-part Battle of Hodenburg Scenario. You can choose to play all seven scenarios in order, but of course you may choose to skip straight to the Battle of Hidenburg if you wish! Equally, any of these scenarios can be used for fun one-off games, outside of a campaign. If doing the latter, you may wish to agree with your opponent which player will be the Attacker and who will be the Defender, as often this will affect army composition. If you and your opponent cannot agree, you can always roll off to decide.

Scenario 1 - A Desperate Dash

A halfling scouting force has discovered a large contingent of Riftforged amassing on the edges of the Shires and has lured a portion of their forces away, where they can be intercepted in the Bogs by another halfling force from nearby Abbetshire.

Force Composition

Both players select armies of 750 points each with the following additional constraints

- No unit may cost over 250 points (including artefacts)
- Maximum 2 Heroes per army
- Maximum 1 War Engine per army
- Maximum 1 unit with the Fly special rule per army

The Table

You should play this game on a 4' x 4' sized table.

Terrain

To represent the swampy Bogs, it is recommended that you use at least four pieces of Height 0 Difficult Terrain, with each piece more than 6" from another.

Scenario Special Rules

To represent the scouting abilities of the halfling vanguard, the Riftforged player must begin deployment first. The Riftforged player may then choose whether to take the first Turn of the game. Roll for Scout as normal.

Conditions of Victory

At the end of the game, add up the points cost of all of the Enemy units you Routed. That is your score. Your opponent does the same and you compare scores.

If the difference between the scores in favour of a player is at least 10% of the total cost of the armies, that player wins; otherwise the game is a draw.

SCENARIO 2 - BATTLE IN THE WOLDS

The plucky halflings have scattered the initial Riftforged forces, but another horde of Riftforged have stuck into the Northwolds, where they are met by stubborn resistance from the resilient hill-folk.

The player that won the previous scenario is considered to be the Attacker in this scenario.

Force Composition

Both players select armies of 1,000 points each, using the normal army composition rules.

The Table

You should play this game on a 6' x 4' sized table.

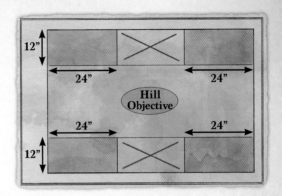

Terrain

To represent the terrain in the Northwolds, use at least three large hills, with one placed directly in the centre of the board.

Scenario Special Rules

Divide the players' usual deployment zones into three sections, each 24" across. No units may be deployed in the central section of either zone. The Defender player may choose which side of the table they deploy on.

Conditions of Victory

At the end of the game, add up the Unit Strength of all of your units that have the majority of their footprint on the hill in the centre of the playing area. That is your Victory Point (VP) score. Your opponent does the same and you compare scores. The player with the most VPs is the winner.

SCENARIO 3 - A SOLID DEFENCE

If the Riftforged rampage is succeeding, the halflings need to muster a force at the border to defend a set of guardburgs and repulse the invaders.

If the Riftforged are on the back foot, the halflings must attempt to destroy a number of crude constructions which the Riftforged appear to be using to boost their arcane power.

The player that won the previous scenario is considered to be the Attacker in this scenario.

Force Composition

The Attacker selects an army of 1,500 points, using the normal army composition rules.

The Defender selects an army of 1,000 points, using the normal army composition rules.

The Table

You should play this game on a 6' x 4' sized table.

Terrain

The only Blocking Terrain used in this scenario should be the three pieces identified below.

Scenario Special Rules

After choosing sides, the Defender must place three pieces of Height 6 Blocking Terrain in their half of the board, but outside of their Deployment Zone. These pieces of terrain represent either the Riftforged power constructs, or the halfling guardburgs as appropriate. They should each be roughly 4" square. They function as Objective Markers for the purposes of this scenario. When controlled by the Attacking player at the end of a Turn, an Objective Marker may be destroyed. If destroyed, remove the piece of terrain from the table.

Conditions of Victory

If the Attacker is able to destroy all three of the Objectives they will win the scenario. Any other result is a win for the Defender.

SCENARIO 4 - IN DEEP WATER

The Halflings begin the muster at Hodenburg, preparing for an all-out onslaught by the Riftforged invaders. To delay the inevitable siege, the halflings divert forces to the Tanmill Canal, knowing that the Riftforged will likely follow it all the way to the city walls.

The player that won the previous scenario is the Attacker in this scenario.

Force Composition

The Attacker selects an army of 2,000 points, using the normal army composition rules.

The Defender selects an army of 1,500 points, using the normal army composition rules.

The Table

You should play this game on a 6' x 4' sized table.

Terrain

Place a suitable river or canal from one of the long board edges to the other, along the centre line of the table. The canal is considered to be Flat Difficult Terrain. Place other terrain as desired.

Conditions of Victory

The Attacker must have more Unit Strength in the section of the table shown on the map than the Defender to win. Any other outcome is a victory for the Defender.

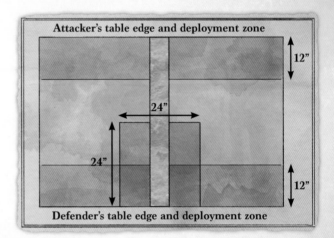

THE BATTLE OF HODENBURG

The Battle of Hodenburg is a three-part scenario that can be played either as three separate games, or may follow on from the previous scenarios and be played in order.

SCENARIO 5 - THE BATTLE OF THE GREAT HEATH

Realising that the Riftforged may be drawing power from smashing at the city walls, the halflings open the gates and hope to spring an ambush on the orcs heading to the Great Heath, an enormous garden in the middle of the city.

If playing as part of the larger campaign, the winner of the previous scenario is considered to be the Attacker in this game.

The Attacker may choose any of the scenarios detailed in the Kings of War rulebook.

Force Composition

Agree how many points both players have to spend (they both get the same amount). It is recommended that players have at least 2,000 points each to spend.

The Table

You should play this game on a 6' x 4' sized table.

Terrain

Place 3-4 small buildings round the edge of the table (within 3" of the edges). Use small Difficult terrain (woods) and some Obstacles (hedges) to represent the gardens in the rest of the battlefield.

SCENARIO 6 - THE RAID ON THE GRAINBARN

A large portion of the Riftforged force have found tunnels beneath the city that they are using to access parts of the city that would otherwise be inaccessible.

The player that won the previous scenario is the Attacker in this scenario.

Force Composition

Agree how many points both players have to spend (they both get the same amount). It is recommended that players have at least 1,500 points each to spend.

The Table

You should play this game on a 6' x 4' sized table.

Terrain

Use terrain that represents a large open dungeon-like space under the city. Use lots of rocks, ruined walls and blocking terrain to create the environment.

Scenario Special Rules

This game is played lengthways on the table, as shown on the map. Additionally, to represent the gloomy conditions of the underground battle, all Ranged Attacks and Spells that target enemy units suffer an additional -1 to-hit modifier. The Attacker may decide whether to take the first or second Turn.

Conditions of Victory

The Attacker must have more Unit Strength in the section of the table shown on the map than the Defender to win. Any other outcome is a victory for the Defender.

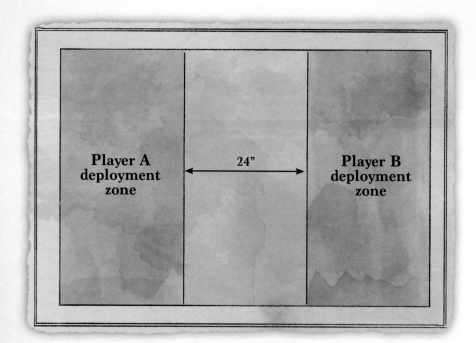

SCENARIO 7 - THE FIGHT FOR HODENBURG SQUARE

This is it, the last stand at Hodenburg for one of these forces. Perhaps the Riftforged have managed to surround the last of the halfling defenders, or maybe the halflings have cut off and trapped a large portion of the Riftforged forces in the middle of the city and must destroy them before reinforcements arrive!

The player that won the previous scenario is the Attacker in this scenario.

Force Composition

Agree how many points both players have to spend (they both get the same amount). It is recommended that players have at least 2,000 points each to spend. The Attacker then gets an additional 25% (e.g. if the Defender has 2,000 points, the attacker will get 2,500).

The Table

You should play this game on a 6' x 4' sized table.

Terrain

Place 2-3 small buildings round the edge of the table (within 3" of the edges). Use 1-2 more small buildings and some walls in the rest of the battlefield to represent Hodenburg Square.

Scenario Special Rules

This game is played lengthways on the table, as shown on the map. The Attacker has two Deployment Zones, one at each end of the table, whilst the Defender may deploy anywhere within 12" of the centre line drawn between the two long board edges. The defender places three Objective Markers anywhere along this centre line, before rolling to see who deploys first.

Conditions of Victory

The player who controls the most Objective Markers at the end of the game wins the Scenario and the campaign.

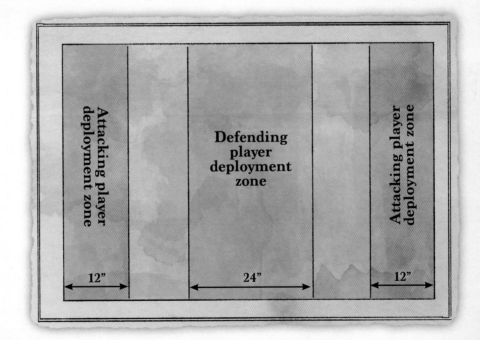

HALFLINGS

PIERSON BLYTHE
TANMILL LAB ENGINEER

The Army of the Shires

The halflings would be the first to admit that they are not natural soldiers. The don't have a lust for blood like the orcs, they don't leap into battle over points of offended honour like the dwarfs, nor do they feel a thrill over the pomp and glory of an army with banners like many humans and even elves. Halflings are far more interested in tinkering in their workshops, reaping bountiful harvests, and sharing a good meal, good ale, and perhaps a relaxing smoke with family and friends. Many outsiders often mistake the halflings as weak and cowardly because of this outwardly good nature.

In this they are gravely mistaken. Because, while the halflings do love the pleasures of life, they are willing to go to great lengths to protect those things from anyone they think might be trying to take them away. They will defend their own with a savagery and viciousness that have taken many by surprise – and to their fatal cost. They can be kind, gentle and generous, but equally cold, pragmatic, and utterly ruthless.

During their wandering days of old, every halfling had to be ready to pick up a weapon to protect their family. Once settled in the Shires, they realised they needed a real army to defend themselves. For the most part they copied the sort of armies they saw in the world around them, with infantry, cavalry and artillery, but as with most things they gave it a unique halfling twist.

The armies of the Shires have changed with time and circumstances but the present organisation is a well-balanced one that commands respect from friend and foe alike. To counter their obvious limitations over other races such as humans, elves and orcs, the largest halflings are encouraged to sign up to the military to serve in the guardburgs or other divisions of the army. Some impressive individuals can reach the giddy heights of four and a half feet tall.

Like many armies, much of a halfling army is composed of infantry. Medium and light soldiers are the most common, although they also have a solid core of heavier troops, plus some unique specialists they can call on. Halfling cavalry is mostly light, but again, there are some heavier mounted troops that can be deployed. In recent years enough of the miniature aralez have been bred as part of an ongoing program, to mount all the halfling cavalry. These valiant creatures are nearly as large as the ponies used previously, but are still suited for a halfling to ride and with their fighting capabilities have made halfling cavalry a near match for larger human cavalry. While the breeding program has not fully replicated the native healing abilities of the larger aralez from the plains, the natural qualities of the smaller breed do retain some of these benefits, protecting their halfling riders from injuries that might otherwise put them down.

Trained Bands

The Trained Bands are the most common troops in the Shire Army. Many so-called braves that are drafted to the Bands are not full-time soldiers, although they are better trained than some militias found elsewhere. They typically have padded leather armour and wooden shields or bucklers, and carry a variety of weapons.

Many Trained Bands use blocks of Spearspikes – spears being an ideal weapon for the small halflings. Their length allow the troops to keep the enemy at a distance and resist cavalry charges. There are also other enthusiastic troops armed with swords, clubs, axes, or even farming tools. They tend to favour close combat, using their small size and quickness to get past the guard of their enemies.

The army is usually preceded by swarms of unarmoured and light infantry brandishing bows, slings, rifles and hand weapons. This vanguard will scout ahead of the main force, killing any game animals (or enemy livestock) they encounter to be collected by the army's cooks following up behind. A Feastmaster is often the leader of these halfling elite scouting warbands. The last thing a marching halfling army wants is to spend the day walking and then have to wait for their food. When the Feastmaster and his gangs are sent ahead to scout for any potential enemies and grab as much food as they can, anything they can trap, shoot and snare gets shoved in the pot. And if they come across any enemies? Well, let's just say people have seen some odd-looking meat in halfling pies.

Some Trained Bands are organised and equipped as light cavalry riding highly trained miniature aralez. Their primary mission is scouting and skirmishing, but on the battlefield they will harass the enemy with ranged fire and protect the army's flanks, charging into melee if absolutely necessary. In training, with their mounts, it has become common for recruits to engage in long races across the plains giving them their nickname of Wild Runners.

Heavy set

Some units of halflings have made soldiering a full-time profession. These Stalwarts are better equipped than the Trained Bands, with metal armour (a mix of thick leather and plate mail), helmets and strong shields. Similar to the Trained Bands, these include blocks of spear-armed infantry that can provide a solid core to a halfling army. Some favour hand weapons, preferring to get in close and personal.

Heavier battle cavalry, mounted on armoured aralez are armed with lances. They are designated as knights by outsiders simply because their weapons, equipment, and battlefield role is similar to the knights of other armies. However, as the halflings have no noble class, the name 'knights' is misleading in the true sense. The halflings themselves know them as Juggers.

Black Powder

In recent years halflings have progressed their adoption of gunpowder weapons, despite their long history of traditional archery. They have found that their short bows, although as powerful as their craft can make them, have trouble penetrating more heavily armoured enemies. After some brief experiments with crossbows, most divisions of the army have begun to switch to muskets and even rifles – an influence surely from their time amongst the armies of the League. Although not as powerful as the shoulder-breaking weapons invented by the dwarfs, they are able to take down most man-sized opponents, despite heavy armour. Whether such weaponry remains in the military domain, or creeps back into the summer sports competitions and everyday rural life, remains to be seen. It is clear though, that the game hunters and poachers that are drafted into military service, or who volunteer themselves outside of the hunting season, are quite taken with them.

Most halfling musketeers are armed with light-weight carbines and can operate either as skirmishers, like their bow-armed comrades, or be used in close formations for concentrated firepower. The dwarfen method of rifling weapons for longer range and better accuracy is a recently imported innovation. But these uncommon, cumbersome and slow-loading rifles are often unsuited for fast-moving light infantry known colloquially in the Shires as "gun-dogs". Thus rifle-armed halflings are used mostly as snipers, in the warbands of the vanguard, or sparingly, massed in formation for long-range firepower.

The Marvels of Tinkering

Halflings have used their mastery of 'tinkering' to devise some truly unique and effective weapons for the battlefield. Some of the most amazing are the flying machines imported from the People of Ej. Those halflings that have settled within the great forest city of the elves and on the rugged slopes of the Blades of Ej are more herders than their crop growing cousins in the Shires. Their technology has combined halfling ingenuity and elven knowhow to create flying machines used for tracking herds and rescuing animals (or people) from high in the treacherous Blades. Aeronaut balloons are able to observe herds from above and reach high places for rescues, while mechanical wings for individuals help them traverse ravines and mountain rivers. These inventions have been adopted by halfling militaries from both the Shire and Ej itself for their obvious tactical and strategic advantages.

Perhaps the most daring troops in a halfling army are therefore the Ej Grenadiers. Using their mechanical-wings, these hot-blooded individuals swoop over the battlefield like birds of prey, raining down destruction with their firebombs before dropping into the midst of the chaos they have created to wreak more destruction. They are supported by the graceful Aeronauts flying in their hot air balloons. Staying high overhead and dropping larger bombs onto the hapless enemies below, their mere presence in the sky can be as much of a psychological threat as a physical one.

War Engines

Most halflings are natural tinkerers with small home workshops where they build various devices 'to make life easier'. Some however, are much more gifted, and produce works of engineering that can arguably match the skills of the dwarfs.

Halflings have created many agricultural machines which have allowed them to grow food more efficiently than almost any other race. The Harvester is a slightly ramshackle crop harvester pressed into combat – a strange mix of wood, metal – and troll. Utilised on the battlefield, it incorporates the cutting devices of a reaping machine and the momentum of a juggernaut fully capable of slicing through enemy troops - like, fittingly, a scythe through ripe wheat.

Originally conceived by the dwarfs as their Steel Behemoth, the concept of an Iron Beast was later brought to the Shires by the halfling Percival Arbuckle and the design later evolved by Paddy Bobart. While the designs of individual machines vary, they are all essentially an enormous four-legged, steam—powered behemoth controlled from a small cabin on the top and armed with guns, piercing tusks and unstoppable momentum. An implacable foe, they are eminently capable of smashing through an enemy army, spreading death and shear panic.

Following their membership of the League, some gunpowder artillery is also used by both the Shire army and also the brigades in Ej, as the – mostly due to exchanges in military hardware. Volley-guns deliver multi-barrelled, devastating close-range fire-power, while the howitzer is a long range cannon capable of firing high explosive projectiles.

Beasts of War

The largest known concentration of forest trolls on the Ardovikian Plain can be found in the Targun Deeps. However, the Forest of Kharne and the swamps to the east of Yangmere are home to small tribes of forest trolls that have migrated from their traditional haunt to find a new home. While most people consider such brutes to be terrifying and stupid beasts, the halflings have, over time, learnt to accommodate and appreciate the presence of the creatures, sometimes trading food and other goods in return for labour. Indeed, some of the most difficult sections of the Tanmill Canal were only possible with the muscle of the trolls. The trolls themselves also love a good fight and in times of need the halflings are able to recruit some of their most willing youngsters with the promise of adventure and the inevitable (although stomach-churning) feast that follows a glorious victory. Their huge strength and toughness makes them a formidable foe—or a very good ally.

Command and Control

Like all armies, the halflings have some commanders, champions and individuals that play unique and crucial roles in keeping the army organised, outwitting the enemy, or just throwing in a lethal surprise.

Sergeants, Constables, Muster Captains and Generals form the main command structures when the halflings march to war. While the goal of halfling leaders is to defend and protect, avoiding conflict where possible, it is the duty of these same leaders to bring the full force of halfling savagery

to the enemy if pushed too far. Once the army engages, keeping the halfling battle lines under control in the face of their anger and desire for relentless revenge can be a daunting and sometimes hopeless task.

Giving the ranks of warriors a distinct advantage are the Saucerors, who can cast magical battle magic like a wizard and also imbue their provisions with the mysterious powers of Gastromancy. This can be a great boon, but there are sometimes horrible side effects. A few unlucky souls become so addicted to it and will stuff themselves to bursting, that they grow into deformed, hideous creatures who will eat quite literally any living thing that cross their paths. Called Greedyguts, these rare abominations are almost uncontrollable and the halflings keep them restrained until they can be turned loose against an enemy on the battlefield where it is hoped they will sate themselves until the next fight.

Legends of the People

From adventurers and warriors, to scholars, merchants and clan leaders, the halflings have many ancestors that have etched their names into the history of the People and into the annals of far-flung places. There are also some halflings whose feats have elevated them to legendary status in recent times.

Born in the Shires, Aeron Cadwallader was educated at the League of Rhordia's College of Warcraft before the Shires seceded their membership of the League. In the brief conflict that followed, Cadwallader demonstrated a remarkable genius for strategy and tactics that ultimately saw the halflings emerge victorious. His knowledge and experience has since been instrumental in expanding, re-shaping and training the armies of the Shires.

Abandoned to the streets at a very young age, the diminutive Ally McSween grew up amongst what polite society might term "the wrong crowd". The bullying of the tiny orphan quickly stopped when the same crowd realised the inherent usefulness of someone half the size of the average man, with tiny hands, and who was incredibly light on their feet. Ally went on to become one the most notorious thieves in Geneza, and as her reputation grew, so did her taste for the high life. This hunger for finer things drove her to become a professional thief, offering her skills to the highest bidder, including, on occasion, the League of Infamy. Her adventures are now legendary and she is frequently the protagonist in many halfling children's games and stories. That she has recently visited both the Shires and Ej on her travels has only helped to swell her adoring fan-base. She has said that she still has a few more years in her before she retires, but is elusive as to her future plans.

Army Special Rules

Alignment: Neutral

Relentless

Once per game, when attacking a unit in melee that currently has at least one point of damage, the unit may reroll up to 3 of the dice that failed to hit.

INFANTRY

Braves

Infantry

Ht 2

Sp 5	Me 5+
Ra -	De 4+

Unit Size	US	Att	Ne	Pts
Regiment (20)	2	12	12/14	80
Horde (40)	3	25	19/21	130
Legion (60)	4	30	25/27	190

Special Rules

Spellward

Options

- Relentless for +5 pts

Keywords: Halfling, Ravenous

Spearspikes

Infantry

Ht 2

Sp 5	Me 5+
Ra -	De 4+

Unit Size	US	Att	Ne	Pts
Regiment (20)	3	15	12/14	100
Horde (40)	4	30	19/21	165

Special Rules

Phalanx, Spellward

Options

- Relentless for +5 pts

Keywords: Halfling, Ravenous

Stalwarts

Infantry

Ht 2

Sp 5	Me 4+
Ra -	De 5+

Unit Size	US	Att	Ne	Pts
Troop (10)	1	10	9/11	75
Regiment (20)	3	12	13/15	115
Horde (40)	4	25	20/22	190

Special Rules

Spellward

Options

- Exchange shields for two-handed weapons, lowering Defence to 4+ and gaining Crushing Strength (1) for free
- Relentless for +5 pts

Keywords: Halfling, Ravenous

RANGED INFANTRY

Poachers
Infantry

Sp	Me	Unit Size	US	Att	Ne	Pts
5	4+	Troop (10)	1	10	9/11	105
Ra	De	Regiment (20)	3	12	13/15	140
5+	3+					

Ht 2

Special Rules
Pathfinder, Scout, Spellward, Stealthy, Vicious (Melee)
Bows: 24"
Options
• Relentless for +5 pts
Keywords: Halfling, Ravenous, Rogue, Tracker

Halfling Rifles
Infantry

Sp	Me	Unit Size	US	Att	Ne	Pts
5	5+	Troop (10)	1	8	8/10	80
Ra	De	Regiment (20)	2	10	12/14	115
5+	3+	Horde (40)	3	20	19/21	200

Ht 2

Special Rules
Spellward
Halfling Rifles: 18", Piercing (1), Steady Aim
Options
• Relentless for +5 pts
Keywords: Halfling, Ravenous, Tinker

CAVALRY

Juggers
Cavalry

Sp	Me	Unit Size	US	Att	Ne	Pts
8	3+	Troop (5)	1	8	10/12	125
Ra	De	Regiment (10)	3	16	13/15	190
-	5+	Horde (20)	4	32	20/22	325

Ht 3

Special Rules
Iron Resolve, Nimble, Thunderous Charge (1), Spellward
Options
• Relentless for +5 pts
Keywords: Aralez, Halfling, Ravenous

Wild Lancers
Cavalry

Sp	Me	Unit Size	US	Att	Ne	Pts
8	3+	Troop (5)	1	7	9/11	100
Ra	De	Regiment (10)	3	14	12/14	155
-	4+	Horde (20)	4	28	19/21	265

Ht 3

Special Rules
Iron Resolve, Nimble, Spellward, Thunderous Charge (1)
Options
• Relentless for +5 pts
Keywords: Aralez, Halfling, Ravenous

Wild Runners
Cavalry

Sp	Me	Unit Size	US	Att	Ne	Pts
8	4+	Troop (5)	1	7	9/11	95
Ra	De	Regiment (10)	2	14	12/14	145
5+	3+					

Ht 3

Special Rules
Iron Resolve, Nimble, Spellward
Shortbows: 18", Steady Aim
Options
• Exchange Shortbows for Blackpowder Weapons: 18", Piercing (1), Steady Aim for [+10/+15] pts
• Relentless for +5 pts
Keywords: Aralez, Halfling, Ravenous

LARGE INFANTRY

Ej Grenadiers*
Large Infantry

Ht 2

Sp	Me	Unit Size	US	Att	Ne	Pts
10	4+	Regiment (3)	2	9	11/13	105
Ra	De					
-	4+					

Special Rules
Brutal (D3), Fly, Nimble
Options
• Relentless for +5 pts
Keywords: Halfling, Tinker

Forest Troll Gunners*
Large Infantry

Ht 3

Sp	Me	Unit Size	US	Att	Ne	Pts
6	4+	Regiment (3)	2	9	12/14	140
Ra	De	Horde (6)	3	18	15/17	230
4+	4+					

Special Rules
Crushing Strength (1), Pathfinder, Regeneration (5+)
Pintle Gun: 18"
Options
• Relentless for +5 pts
Keywords: Halfling, Troll

Forest Trolls
Large Infantry

Ht 3

Sp	Me	Unit Size	US	Att	Ne	Pts
6	4+	Regiment (3)	2	9	12/14	125
Ra	De	Horde (6)	3	18	15/17	205
-	5+					

Special Rules
Crushing Strength (2), Pathfinder, Regeneration (5+)
Keywords: Troll

LARGE CAVALRY

Aeronauts*
Large Cavalry

Ht 5

Sp	Me	Unit Size	US	Att	Ne	Pts
7	4+	Regiment (3)	2	9	13/15	175
Ra	De					
-	5+					

Special Rules
Blast (D3), Crushing Strength (2), Fly, Pathfinder
Bombing Run: In Melee, this unit will always hit the enemy on a 4+ regardless of any other modifiers.
Keywords: Halfling, Tinker

WAR ENGINES

Volley Gun
War Engine

Ht 2

Sp	Me	Unit Size	US	Att	Ne	Pts
5	-	1	0	12	9/11	85
Ra	De					
5+	4+					

Special Rules
Volley Gun: 24", Piercing (2), Reload
Keywords: Artillery, Halfling, Ravenous, Tinker

Howitzer
War Engine

Ht 2

Sp	Me	Unit Size	US	Att	Ne	Pts
5	-	1	0	2	9/11	90
Ra	De					
5+	4+					

Special Rules
Artillery Strike: 48", Blast (D3+1), Ignores Cover, Indirect, Piercing (3), Reload
Keywords: Artillery, Halfling, Ravenous, Tinker

MONSTERS

TITANS

Harvester
Monster (Char)

		Unit Size	US	Att	Ne	Pts	Ht
Sp 5	Me 3+	1	1	D6+8	13/15	140	3
Ra -	De 4+						

Special Rules
Big Shield, Brutal, Crushing Strength (1), Thunderous Charge (1)
Keywords: Halfling, Ravenous, Tinker, Troll

Iron Beast
Titan

		Unit Size	US	Att	Ne	Pts	Ht
Sp 5	Me 4+	1	1	D6+10	16/18	210	5
Ra 4+	De 6+						

Special Rules
Aura: Spellward, Crushing Strength (2), Strider
Halfling Handgun: 18" Att:5, Piercing (1), Steady Aim
Options
- **Pride of the Shires [1]:** This unit gains the Inspiring and Aura (Headstrong) special rule +30 pts

Keywords: Halfling, Ravenous, Tinker

HEROES

Sauceror
Hero (Hv Inf)

		Unit Size	US	Att	Ne	Pts	Ht
Sp 5	Me 5+	1	0	1	9/11	80	2
Ra -	De 4+						

Special Rules
Individual, Spellward
Options
- Mount on a miniature Aralez, increasing Speed to 8 changing to Hero (Cav - Height: 3) for +25 pts

Gastromancy: Unless disordered, immediately before giving this unit a Movement order, pick one of the following Special Rules and roll three dice. If any of the dice score a 4+, apply the Special Rule to this unit. If an (n) value is listed in the Special Rule, (n) is equal to the number of dice rolled that score a 4+.
- Aura (Wild Charge (+n) - **Ravenous** only)
- Aura (Brutal (n) - **Ravenous** only)
- Aura (Lifeleech (+n) - **Ravenous** only)
- Rally (n - **Ravenous** only)

Keywords: Halfling, Ravenous

Engineer
Hero (Inf)

		Unit Size	US	Att	Ne	Pts	Ht
Sp 5	Me 5+	1	0	1	10/12	75	2
Ra 4+	De 4+						

Special Rules
Individual, Inspiring
Halfling Carbine: 18" Piercing (1) Att: 4
Options
- Aura (Wild charge (+1) - **Tinker** only) for 10 pts
- Radiance of Life (**Tinker** only) for +15 pts
- Swap Halfling Carbine for Halfling Long Rifle: Lose Halfling Carbine, gain ranged attack: Ra 3+ - Range 24" Att: 3, Piercing (2) for +15 pts
- **Gadgets and Gizmos [1]:** After both players have deployed, nominate a single core friendly Infantry unit. This unit gains the Tinker keyword and Iron Resolve special rule for +5 pts.

Keywords: Halfling, Tinker

Sergeant
Hero (Inf) | Ht 2

Sp	Me	Unit Size	US	Att	Ne	Pts
5	3+	1	0	3	10/12	55
Ra	De					
-	5+					

Special Rules
Crushing Strength (1), Individual, Inspiring, Spellward
Options
- Mount on a miniature Aralez, increasing Speed to 8 and changing to Hero (Cav - Height: 3) for +25 pts
- Gain Scout for +10 pts. This cannot be in addition to the mount.
- Gain the ranged attack - Bow: 18", Ra: 4+ for +10 pts
- Relentless for +5 pts

The Standard of Hodenburg [1]: This unit gains the Aura (Elite (Melee) - Infantry only) special rule for +25 pts.
Keywords: Halfling, Ravenous

Muster Captain
Hero (Inf) | Ht 2

Sp	Me	Unit Size	US	Att	Ne	Pts
5	3+	1	0	5	12/14	80
Ra	De					
-	5+					

Special Rules
Crushing Strength (1), Individual, Inspiring, Mighty, Spellward
Options
- Mount on a miniature Aralez, increasing Speed to 8 and changing to Hero (Cav - Height: 3) for +35 pts
- Relentless for +5 pts

Keywords: Halfling, Ravenous

Feast Master
Hero (Hv Inf) | Ht 2

Sp	Me	Unit Size	US	Att	Ne	Pts
5	3+	1	0	5	11/13	90
Ra	De					
4+	4+					

Special Rules
Crushing Strength (1), Duelist, Individual, Inspiring, Scout, Spellward
Throwing Cleaver: 12", Piercing (1)
Keywords: Halfling, Ravenous, Rogue, Tracker

Muster Captain on Winged Aralez
Hero (Mon) | Ht 5

Sp	Me	Unit Size	US	Att	Ne	Pts
10	3+	1	1	7	14/16	195
Ra	De					
-	5+					

Special Rules
Crushing Strength (2), Fly, Inspiring, Iron Resolve, Nimble, Spellward, Thunderous Charge (1)
Options
- Relentless for +5 pts

Keywords: Aralez, Halfling, Ravenous

Gunnery Sergeant on Troll
Hero (Lrg Inf) | Ht 3

Sp	Me	Unit Size	US	Att	Ne	Pts
6	3+	1	1	5	13/15	130
Ra	De					
4+	5+					

Special Rules
Crushing Strength (1), Inspiring, Nimble, Pathfinder, Regeneration (5+)
Pintle Gun: Range 18"
Options
- Relentless for +5 pts

Keywords: Halfling, Tinker, Troll

UNIQUE UNITS

Aeron Cadwallader [1]
Hero (Hv Inf) — Ht 2

Sp	Me	Unit Size	US	Att	Ne	Pts
5	3+	1	0	5	13/15	110
Ra	De					
-	5+					

Special Rules
Aura (Nimble - Infantry Only), Crushing Strength (1), Individual, Mighty, Spellward, Very Inspiring
Keywords: Halfling, Ravenous

Greedyguts [1]
Hero (Hv Inf) — Ht 2

Sp	Me	Unit Size	US	Att	Ne	Pts
5	3+	1	0	8	-/16	115
Ra	De					
-	4+					

Special Rules
Crushing Strength (1), Dread, Individual, Lifeleech (3), Wildcharge (D3)
Keywords: Halfling, Mighty, Ravenous

Ally McSween [1]
Hero (Hv Inf) — Ht 2

Sp	Me	Unit Size	US	Att	Ne	Pts
6	3+	1	0	5	11/13	105
Ra	De					
4+	4+					

Special Rules
Crushing Strength (1), Duelist, Individual, Inspiring (self), Scout, Spellward, Stealthy
Throwing Daggers: 12", Piercing (1)
Master Thief: Enemy units within 6" of Ally may not use their Magical Artefact when attacking in combat. When Ally is attacking an enemy unit in combat, she may choose to use a Magical Artefact held by any enemy unit she is engaged with, excluding one use only items.
Keywords: Halfling, Ravenous, Rogue, Tracker

Formation
McSween's Cutthroats

Ally doesn't always work alone. Despite her considerable skills, there are some jobs that require many trusted hands, even if it's just to create a massive distraction by upending a barrel of starving mawpups through the window of the council chambers, or putting a sentry "to sleep".

- 2 Regiments of Poachers (+10pts each)
- Ally McSween (+5 pts)

The Poachers in this formation gain Inspiring (Self) and increase their Range value to 4+

Ally McSween gains Rampage (Melee - D3)

Total Formation cost: +25 pts

RIFTFORGED ORCS

JAARG SKARCRY
TERROR OF THE PLAINS

The Riftforged Legions

Infused with the power of Halpi's Rift, the Riftforged orcs are a breed apart from their green-skinned cousins. Though hunched, they stand as tall as a man, but are considerably broader and well-muscled. Their faces are bestial, with jutting lower jaws and sharp teeth, but these are creatures of brutal intelligence. At first, one might mistake them for a normal orc of Pannithor, but that illusion is soon dispelled. Their armour and weaponry is newly forged and meticulously maintained. The energy from which they were forged can barely be contained, manifesting itself in their glowing eyes and flickering electrical energy that crackles across their bodies whenever they are roused to war. They are the children of the storm, and the march of their legions is preceded by black thunderclouds and coruscating lightning.

Each Riftforged legion is an autonomous fighting force, disciplined and well-drilled. A campaigning legion might have as few as a hundred warriors at its disposal, or as many as two thousand – the number depends upon the success of its commanders, for Garkan grants reinforcements more readily to those legions who bring him the most glory in battle.

Stormbringers

Riftforged legions are organised into cohorts, each led by a Stormbringer – an orc of exceptional power and cunning, whose exposure to rift-energy has increased their physical strength, while often leaving them hideously scarred. Stormbringers are the foci of the legions – while but one of them draws breath, the power of the storm still rages, energising the horde. Such power makes the Stormbringers fiercely competitive and arrogant, ever ready to challenge their opponents to single combat in an effort not only to display their supremacy, but to tear the heart from the enemy force. The greatest Stormbringers are hulking specimens, their flesh charred and cracked, their armour gilded and embellished by Abyssal smiths in recognition of their might, and their rune-cursed hammers channelling the power of the storm to smite their foes.

And yet the Stormbringers were once ordinary legionaries – this power grows with age, experience, and success in battle – the energy within each Riftforged orc is a raging torrent, always threatening to overwhelm the weak. All Stormbringers are promoted from within the ranks – the very first of their number having led their brethren out of the Abyss. Should a Stormbringer show any sign of weakness, they can expect to be quickly dethroned by another aspirant, ensuring that the Riftforged legions are always led by the strongest and most merciless warriors.

Many Stormbringers ride to war on a monstrous mount – the most vicious and wild-spirited beast they can find. Riftforged orcs have a particular affinity for manticores, which they first faced in the mountains of Tragar shortly after leaving the Abyss. However, when the Stormbringers first encountered tribes of normal orcs, they paid begrudging respect to those orc Krudgers who had managed to tame massive, bad-tempered Slashers, and determined to find such a beast for themselves.

Soldiers of the Legion

The mainstay of the legions are the Riftforged legionaries themselves. These disciplined, heavily muscled orcs were created for war. When not fighting, they train relentlessly, until their weapon drills are as practised and instinctive as they are devastating. In battle, any similarity between a legionary and a common orc is quickly dispelled. Besides their fearsome appearance, their perfectly maintained armour, weapons, and near-mechanical combat manoeuvres speak of highly trained, professional soldiers rather than marauding warbands.

Riftforged Legionaries are organised into cohorts, each containing several regiments of these drilled warriors. A legionary regiment will be equipped either with hammers and shields, or great-hammers. The former are tasked with holding the line in a near-unbreakable shieldwall, while the latter form units of shock troops – quite literally, given the elementally charged energy that builds around the regiments as the fighting escalates.

The creation of a Riftforged legionary is no easy task. Each must be flesh-forged within the Abyss, and thus it can take considerable time for a legion to receive reinforcements while on campaign. As a result, though they are almost without fear, no legionary will sell their life cheaply. That's where the unforged orc regiments come into their own. These common orcs follow the legions in great numbers, awestruck by the sheer power of their larger cousins, and desperate to take their place amongst the ranks. They race into battle as berserkers, performing reckless but devastating charges to soften the enemy lines, selling their lives so that the legionaries might notice their skill and bravery. If the Youngax aspirants had any idea of the true cost of being torn apart

and reconstituted as a Riftforged Orc, they might perhaps think twice. But for most, any price is worth paying for the chance at such awesome power.

Those legions who ventured to the frozen north found common orcs in shorter supply. Instead, the adaptable Riftforged orcs took their cue from the Northern Alliance, who use ravening beasts as their army's vanguard. The Stormbringers of the northern legions sent hunting parties in search of vicious Tundra Wolves, and began to train packs of the swift brutes to direct into battle. The job of rearing and training Tundra Wolves generally falls to those Legionary veterans who have been too badly injured in battle to fight effectively – serving the legion as a packmaster is a fate far more preferable to being served up as campaign rations.

Death from Above!

The elite warriors of the legion, who have proven themselves many times in battle, are often formed into hard-hitting Helstriker units. Initiation into these savage airborne cavalry units is an ordeal in itself, for the chosen legionary must first select their mount from the legion's winged manticores. These beasts, captured in the mountains of Tragar, are renowned for their strength and ferocity, and breaking them into domesticity is virtually impossible. The only way to win the respect of such a monster is to dominate it with force of will, or a feat of brute strength, after which the manticore will – usually – accept the orc as its master. The potentate Helstrikers draw lots to see who will choose their future mount first. This is a dubious honour, for honour dictates that the orc must pick the biggest and most belligerent beast of those available. Many an orc has lost a limb in the attempt, making them fit for little other than rearing fledgling manticores, or exiling themselves from the legion in shame.

In battle, Helstrikers are tasked with swooping over the enemy ranks, causing as much disruption as possible by tearing apart enemy wizards, artillery teams and commanders, before launching devastating charges into the rear of larger formations, putting even the most powerful foes to flight.

Service in a Helstrike squadron is seen as the true proving ground for future Stormbringers. As such, it is no wonder that the strongest Riftforged Orcs are given such a dangerous role – it is a way of both reducing the pool of potential rivals through untimely death in battle, and also of ensuring that only the very best contenders survive to take up the mantle of Stormbringer, and thus add to the legion's legacy.

Call the Storm

The relationship between the Riftforged Orcs and their god, Garkan, is more direct and pragmatic than spiritual. Garkan created the Riftforged legions in the Abyss – many of the Stormbringers alive today stood in Garkan's august dark presence as he issued their first commands. He imbued each legionary with the power of the Nexus – the great Rift of Halpi – which even now allows the horde to summon forth roiling storms as they join battle.

So it is that the spiritual leaders of the Riftforged Orcs are not mere priests or double-speaking shamans, but living embodiments of their patron's power, whose toil at sacred elemental forges, or unto the anvil of battle, is a homage to the power of Garkan himself.

Some of these orcs are known as Stormcallers, and it is they who, through visions given to them by their patron Wicked One, summon the greatest storms that herald the arrival of the legion. The Stormcallers stand apart from the hierarchy of any one legion, forming their own conclave beneath Garkan's rule. They act as messengers and emissaries, often delivering the orders of the High Marshalls or even one of the Wicked Ones directly from the Abyss to the field of battle. Although none amongst the Riftforged would openly question the Stormcallers' authority, the legionaries are always uneasy around the enigmatic individuals, whose nature seems disturbingly similar to the Wicked Ones themselves.

There are also the Riftforgers – silent, sombre individuals at odds with the bombastic Stormcallers. Often the only sound that marks their passing is the repeated monotone clang of metal striking metal as they forge the unseen power that surrounds the legions. Each strike of the hammer empowers the Riftforged with crackling energies, strengthening their forms and striking down their foes. The rings of the Riftforgers are also responsible for maintaining the Riftforged armour and weapons. Each piece of enchanted artifice is beyond the understanding of most mortal smiths, but the Riftforgers are blessed with the dark skills of their patron.

They will often accompany the legions to battle to see their master's orders fulfilled, usually upon a huge, floating Stormforged Shrine – an elemental forge, from where the Riftforger strikes ritual runes, harnessing the power of the storm to destroy the enemy or bolster the legion's strength.

Elemental Might

The power of Halpi's Rift allowed Garkan to create the Riftforged Legions, but though these new orcs were his greatest success, they were not the only creation to come from his experimentations with the Nexus of Power.

The Thunderseers are abominations, crafted from cyclopes, their souls fragmented by exposure to the Nexus. They are tortured creatures, driven almost to the brink of madness by their gift of foresight. An eternity of torment in the Abyss is a terrible fate for most mortals, but for the cyclopes, who always see a few moments into their own futures, the horror is almost unimaginable – to know what they must endure is like living through it twice over. These shattered souls were plucked from damnation by Garkan, and fused with the same elemental energy of the Riftforged Orcs. The Thunderseers, as they are now known, are hulking creatures, revered and respected by the legionaries, for their gift of foresight makes them as adept at battle-strategy as they are at tearing apart the enemy with their massive strength.

Stormslayers, by contrast, lack any subtlety or guile. These massive creatures were created from the same stock as trolls, but exposure to the Nexus of Power drove them to a rage-fuelled frenzy. The lightning that arced around their hulking bodies was so powerful that most succumbed to the pain, and Garkan nearly discarded all of them as a failed experiment. Yet a few survived through sheer bloody-mindedness, and these Garkan saved. The Wicked One forged for each of them a pair of great falchions, with which they could control the lightning that might otherwise consume them. In battle, the Stormslayers are driven by pain-fuelled rage, and with each sweep of their falchions the foe are smote with the very force of the storm.

The Ambarox are a true oddity. No one is certain whether they were created by Garkan at all. Rather, drawn to the lightning upon which they seem to feed, these large, insectoid creatures burrowed out of their subterranean lairs when the Riftforged Orcs emerged from the Abyss. Their bony protrusions are able to channels lightning into their own bodies, causing them to glow and crackle with barely controllable energy, and then discharge it at the foe in powerful blasts. The Riftforged legions view these creatures as heralds of Garkan, and treat them with great reverence, but whether they are truly creations of the Wicked Ones, or simply symbiotic creatures following a source of food, none can really be sure.

The last of Garkan's Riftforged creations, and the fewest in number, are the Storm Giants. Not only is the process of forging such a titanic being a truly gargantuan task, but the power required is so vast that the capping of the Nexus made it impossible to ever create more of their kind. Thankfully for Garkan – and the Storm Giants themselves – they are incredibly long-lived and very hard to kill. Possessed of the same uncanny elemental powers as the legions they follow, Storm Giants bestride the battlefield like gods of old, unleashing bolts of lightning with every crushing blow from their massive hammers, their baleful eyes brimming with the redolent energy of the rift that birthed them.

Army Special Rule
Alignment: Evil

Stormstrike

Any natural rolls of 6 to hit are resolved with the Blast (2) special rule. This effect does not work if the unit needs more than a 6 to hit.

Army Special Rules

The Riftforged Orc list is a Theme List. The Master List for this Theme is Orcs.

The following units may be taken from the Master List:
Skulks*, Morax, Gore Riders, Orclings*, Flagger, Fight Wagons

In addition to units from the Master List, Riftforged Orc armies may select from the following units.

INFANTRY

Unforged Orcs
Heavy Infantry
Ht 2

Sp	Me	Unit Size	US	Att	Ne	Pts
5	4+	Regiment (20)	3	12	13/15	115
Ra	De	Horde (40)	4	25	20/22	190
-	4+					

Special Rules
Crushing Strength (1)
Keywords: Orc

Riftforged Legionaries
Heavy Infantry
Ht 2

Sp	Me	Unit Size	US	Att	Ne	Pts
5	3+	Troop (10)	1	10	10/12	100
Ra	De	Regiment (20)	3	12	14/16	150
-	5+	Horde (40)	4	25	21/23	250

Special Rules
Crushing Strength (1)
Keywords: Riftforged

Reborn Legionaries*
Heavy Infantry
Ht 2

Sp	Me	Unit Size	US	Att	Ne	Pts
5	3+	Troop (10)	1	10	11/13	120
Ra	De	Regiment (20)	3	12	15/17	185
-	5+					

Special Rules
Crushing Strength (2) Inspiring
Keywords: Riftforged

Riftwalkers*
Heavy Infantry
Ht 2

Sp	Me	Unit Size	US	Att	Ne	Pts
7	4+	Troop (10)	1	10	-/12	120
Ra	De	Regiment (20)	3	12	-/16	185
-	5+					

Special Rules
Crushing Strength (1), Fly, Nimble, Strider
Keywords: Riftforged

CAVALRY

Tundra Wolves*
Cavalry

Ht 2

Sp 9	Me 3+	Unit Size	US	Att	Ne	Pts
Ra -	De 4+	Troop (5)	1	9	10/12	115
		Regiment (10)	3	18	13/15	180

Special Rules
Nimble, Thunderous Charge (1)
Keywords: Beast, Tundra Wolf

LARGE CAVALRY

Helstrikers
Large Cavalry

Ht 4

Sp 10	Me 3+	Unit Size	US	Att	Ne	Pts
Ra -	De 5+	Regiment (3)	2	9	12/14	160
		Horde (6)	3	18	15/17	265

Special Rules
Brutal, Crushing Strength (1), Fly, Lifeleech (1), Thunderous Charge (1)
Keywords: Riftforged, Manticore

TITANS

Storm Giant
Titan

Ht 6

Sp 7	Me 4+	Unit Size	US	Att	Ne	Pts
Ra -	De 5+	1	1	D6+8	18/20	240

Special Rules
Brutal, Cloak of Death, Crushing Strength (4), Slayer (Melee - D6), Strider
Spells
Windblast (6)
Keywords: Giant, Riftforged

Stormforged Shrine [1]
Titan, Spellcaster: 2

Ht 4

Sp 5	Me 4+	Unit Size	US	Att	Ne	Pts
Ra -	De 5+	1	1	8	-/17	240

Special Rules
Aura (Fury), Crushing Strength (1), Inspiring
Anvil of the Rift: After successfully casting Bane Chant or Host Shadowbeast, the Stormforged Shrine may choose to cast either spell again with 1 less die on another appropriate Riftforged unit within 12" regardless of Line of Sight. This may continue until a casting is failed, no unit may be targeted twice with the same spell.
Power of the Rift: For each other friendly core Riftforged unit within 6", increase the amount of dice rolled with Bane Chant, Host Shadowbeast, Lightning Bolt by 1 to a maximum bonus of +3
Spells
Bane Chant (1), Host Shadowbeast (4), Lightning Bolt (3)
Note: Base size cannot be increased beyond 75x75mm
Keywords: Riftforged, Shrine

MONSTROUS INFANTRY

Thunderseers
Monstrous Infantry

Ht 3

Sp 6	Me 4+	Unit Size	US	Att	Ne	Pts
Ra -	De 5+	Regiment (3)	2	15	12/14	135
		Horde (6)	3	30	15/17	225

Special Rules
Crushing Strength (1), Pathfinder, Spellward
Options
• **Visions from the Rift:** May take **Visions from the Rift** [2] for 10 points.
After deployment and all Scout moves have been completed by both players, but before rolling for first turn, this unit may be picked up and redeployed anywhere in the controlling players deployment zone.
Keywords: Cyclopes, Riftforged

MONSTERS

Stormslayer
Monster

Ht 3

Sp	Me	Unit Size	US	Att	Ne	Pts
7	3+	1	1	8	-/14	130
Ra	De					
-	4+					

Special Rules
Crushing Strength (2), Nimble
Keywords: Riftforged, Troll

Ambarox
Monster

Ht 3

Sp	Me	Unit Size	US	Att	Ne	Pts
5	4+	1	1	3	10/12	115
Ra	De					
4+	4+					

Special Rules
Nimble
Energy Blast: 24", Blast (D3), Piercing (1), Steady Aim
Keywords: Insectoid

HEROES

Stormbringer
Hero (Hv Inf)

Ht 2

Sp	Me	Unit Size	US	Att	Ne	Pts
5	3+	1	0	5	13/15	100
Ra	De					
-	5+					

Special Rules
Crushing Strength (2), Individual, Inspiring, Mighty
Options
• Upgrade with Mount, increasing Speed to 8 and changing to Hero (Cav - Height: 3) for +35 pts
• Stormstrike for +10 pts
Keywords: Riftforged

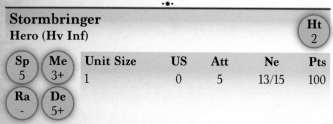

Riftforger
Hero (Hv Inf), Spellcaster: 0

Ht 2

Sp	Me	Unit Size	US	Att	Ne	Pts
5	3+	1	0	3	10/12	50
Ra	De					
-	5+					

Special Rules
Arcane Smithy, Crushing Strength (2), Individual
Arcane Smithy: This unit may cast their Bane Chant or Host Shadow Beast spell while engaged with an enemy unit. If they do so, the Riftforger may ONLY target themselves, or another qualifying Friendly Core unit engaged with the same enemy unit as the Riftforger regardless of Line of Sight.
Options
• Upgrade with a Mount, increasing Speed to 8 and changing to Hero (Cav - Height: 3) for +25 pts
• Bane Chant (2) for +25 pts
• Host Shadowbeast (6) for +25 pts
• Stormstrike for +10 pts
Keywords: Riftforged

Stormcaller
Hero (Hv Inf), Spellcaster: 2

Ht 2

Sp	Me	Unit Size	US	Att	Ne	Pts
5	4+	1	0	1	11/13	85
Ra	De					
-	5+					

Special Rules
Crushing Strength (1), Individual
Spells
Lightning Bolt (4)
Options
• Upgrade with a Mount, increasing Speed to 8 and changing to Hero (Cav – Height: 3) for +25 pts
• Icy Breath (8) for +25 pts, or free if it replaces Lightning Bolt
• Bane Chant (2) for +20 pts
• [1] Blizzard (3) for +40 pts
• [1] Veil of Shadows (3) for +30 pts
Keywords: Riftforged

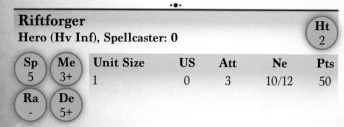

RIFTFORGED ORCS

Stormbringer on Winged Slasher
Hero (Titan)

Ht						6

Sp	Me	Unit Size	US	Att	Ne	Pts
10	3+	1	1	10	17/19	295
Ra	De					
4+	5+					

Special Rules
Crushing Strength (3), Fly, Fury, Inspiring, Nimble
Stormbreath: 12", Steady Aim
Keywords: Draconic, Riftforged

Stormbringer on Helstrike Manticore
Hero (Lrg Cav)

Ht						4

Sp	Me	Unit Size	US	Att	Ne	Pts
10	3+	1	1	5	13/15	160
Ra	De					
-	5+					

Special Rules
Brutal, Crushing Strength (2), Fly, Inspiring, Lifeleech (1), Nimble
Keywords: Riftforged, Manticore

UNIQUE UNITS

Vohdler [1]
Hero (Mon Inf)

Ht						3

Sp	Me	Unit Size	US	Att	Ne	Pts
6	3+	1	1	7	-/15	190
Ra	De					
-	6+					

Special Rules
Crushing Strength (2), Inspiring, Nimble, Pathfinder, Spellward
Visions from the Rift: After deployment and all Scout moves have been completed by both players, but before rolling for first turn, this unit may be picked up and redeployed anywhere in the controlling players deployment zone.
Grand Seer: The [2] restriction for Visions from the Rift is lifted from any army that includes Vohdler.
Keywords: Cyclopes, Riftforged

Thonaar [1]
Hero (Cav)

Ht						3

Sp	Me	Unit Size	US	Att	Ne	Pts
8	3+	1	0	6	14/16	170
Ra	De					
-	5+					

Special Rules
Crushing Strength (2), Individual, Inspiring, Mighty, Stormstrike, Thunderstruck.
Thunderstruck: Thonaar's Stormstrike ability triggers on rolls of 5+. In addition, if an enemy is damaged by Thonaar's Stormstrike attack, that enemy suffers -1 to its hit rolls during its next turn.
Keywords: Riftforged

Formation

The Iron Boots

The Iron Boots, led by Jourk Bludmaw, have seen extensive action against Ratkin infestations east of Zarak and also along the coastline of the Frozen Sea, delighting in smashing and looting the fishing towns of the northern tribes. They've even harassed and continue to fight ongoing battles against the nomadic ogres on the Mammoth Steppe, as they slowly march west, keen on establishing a base in the Howling Peaks.

- 2 regiments of Riftforged Legionaries (+5 pts each)

- 1 regiment of Reborn Legionaries (+20 pts)

All units in this formation increase their Waver and Rout Nerve values by +1. The Reborn Legionaries in this formation gain Aura (Wild Charge D3 - **Orc** only).

Total Formation cost: +30 pts

59

Clash Of Kings Updates 2022

While Kings of War is a well-balanced wargame, no game is absolutely perfect. As has become tradition for the game, you will find a range of game and unit updates on the following pages. We've put in a lot this time – so this is a bumper update that we hope players will love.

We recommend implementing all the following rule and unit changes to keep the game as fresh and balanced as possible.

Changes to Existing Special Rules

Ignores Cover

The firing unit only suffers cover penalties for units that have at least half their base within Difficult Terrain. Note that the firing unit still needs to have Line of Sight to the target to fire at it.

Inspiring (x) and Very Inspiring (x)

In all instances where a unit has the Inspiring (x) or Very Inspiring (x) special rule, change it to Inspiring or Very Inspiring respectively, with the exception of Inspiring (Self).

New Special Rules

Rampage (n)

When attacking an enemy unit with the Infantry, Heavy Infantry, Swarm or Cavalry unit type, a unit with this Special Rule gains (n) additional attacks on its profile until the end of the Turn.

Slayer (n)

When attacking an enemy unit with the Large Infantry, Monstrous Infantry, Large Cavalry, Monster or Titan unit types, a unit with this Special Rule gains (n) additional attacks on its profile until the end of the Turn.

Spellward

All spells, both Friendly and Enemy, targeting this unit suffer a -1 to hit modifier. Note that rolls of natural unmodified 6s still always hit.

Formations

One of the things we always intended to reintroduce to the game was the concept of Formations. We know many players will be excited for this! Formations are thematic groups of units that, when taken and used together, gain certain bonuses during a game. This represents the units being especially effective in combination, or having years of training and experience working and fighting together. They are also a great excuse for modelling and naming your units, and building stories around them.

When using Formations in an army, the following rules apply:

- Units may not count towards more than one Formation at a time.

- When taking a Formation, all units in the Formation must be taken to gain any listed upgrades (you cannot partially field a Formation!).

- The number in brackets listed for units in Formations represents the number of additional points they cost, in addition to their initial value.

- Unless indicated otherwise, units in Formations may take magical artefacts, following the usual rules for doing so.

- Formations may not be taken as Allies.

- Each Formation is unique and so may not be taken more than once in an army.

CHANGES TO EXISTING SPELLS

Fireball

Add 'Shattering' as a modifier.

Hex

Amend to read; "Instead of causing damage, if one or more hits are scored, the target enemy unit is Hexed and receives two points of damage each time it scores a hit with a spell until the end of its next Turn. A Nerve test is not required for damage caused by this spell.

While a unit is Hexed, it may not cast spells unless it received a Halt or Change Facing order in the Movement Phase."

Enthral

Remove the line "A unit can only be targeted by Enthral once per turn".

Mindfog

Add 'Shattering' as a modifier.

ARCANE ABILITIES

Non-Living Legend heroes with a spellcaster tier of 1 or more may purchase any of the following upgrades:

Knowledgeable [1]. 10 pts. The hero's spellcaster tier is increased by one, to a maximum of three.

Incantation of the Tempest [1]. 10 pts. Before casting any spells, this model may roll a single die. On a result of 4+, this model may reroll any misses on spells it casts this Turn. If the model does not roll a 4+, it is instead Disordered and cannot cast any spells for the remainder of the Turn.

NEW ARMY COMPOSITION RULES

Allied units may never take unique or limited upgrades.

LIBRARY OF ARCANE KNOWLEDGE

In addition to the spells listed on their profile, a non-Living Legend unit with a spellcaster tier of 1 or more may purchase spells from the Library of Arcane Knowledge below. Any army may purchase each spell listed in the library once, and for a unit in addition to any artefacts or other selections on that unit's profile (including optional upgrades) that are available.

A spellcaster can only purchase a version of the spell up to their spellcaster level; it can purchase below its level, but not above. i.e., a tier 1 spellcaster can purchase tier 1 spells, but not tier 2 or 3; whereas a tier 3 spellcaster can purchase tier 1, 2 and 3 spells.

For example, a tier 2 spellcaster can purchase Mindfog (2) for 10 points, or Mindfog (3) for 15 points, but not Mindfog (4).

For example, spellcasters of tiers 2 and 3 can purchase Barkskin [1] (5) for 25 points, but as this is the only version of this spell, it is not available for spellcaster with a lower tier.

Spell name	Range	Targets	Effect	Modifiers	Spellcaster Tier (n) value and Points Cost		
					1	2	3
Mindfog	36"	Enemy	Instead of causing damage, if one or more hits are scored, make a Nerve test for the target at the end of the Ranged phase as though damage had been caused.	Shattering	(2) for 10pts	(3) for 15pts	(4) for 20pts
Hex	30"	Enemy	Instead of causing damage, if one or more hits are scored, the target enemy unit is Hexed and receives two points of damage each time it scores a hit with a spell until the end of its next Turn. A Nerve test is not required for damage caused by this spell. While a unit is Hexed, it may not cast spells unless it received a Halt or Change Facing order in the Movement Phase.	-	(2) for 15pts	(3) for 20pts	-
Veil of Shadows [1]	-	Self	If one or more hits are scored, the spellcaster gains the Aura (Stealthy) special rule until the start of the player's next Turn.	-	(2) for 25pts	(3) for 30pts	(4) for 35pts
Celestial Restoration [1]	36"	Friendly, CC	For each hit scored roll a single D3 and total the results. The unit regains this many points of damage that it has previously suffered.	Indirect	-	(2) for 25pts	(3) for 35pts

Spell name	Range	Targets	Effect	Modifiers	Spellcaster Tier (n) value and Points Cost		
					1	2	3
Barskin [1]	12"	Friendly, Self, CC	Unlike most spells that always hit on a 4+, this spell rolls to hit on a result equal to the target's Defence value (e.g. when targeting a Defence 5 unit, the spell will hit on a 5+ before any other modifiers are applied). For each hit scored, place a Barkskin token on the target unit (use a different coloured die or suitable markers). Whenever a unit with one or more Barkskin tokens would suffer damage, it instead removes one Barkskin token per point of damage taken. Once all Barkskin tokens have been removed, excess damage is suffered by the unit as normal. Removing a Barkskin token does not count as taking damage for the purposes of requiring a Nerve test or other special rules, but will still Disorder the target if the token was removed in Melee. At the start of the caster's following Turn, all remaining Barkskin tokens on the target unit are removed from play.	-	-	(5) for 25pts	-
Alchemist's Curse [1]	12"	Enemy	Add the target's Defence value to the (n) value of this spell. *e.g. Casting Alchemist's Curse [1] (2) against a Defence 4+ unit, will result in Alchemist's Curse [1] (6), rolling 6 dice for the spell.*	Piercing (4), Hits on a 5+ against units in Cover	(0) for 15pts	(2) for 25pts	(4) for 35pts

Spell name	Range	Targets	Effect	Modifiers	Spellcaster Tier (n) value and Points Cost		
					1	2	3
Wither and Perish	12"	Enemy, CC	If one or more hits are scored, the target unit has a -1 modifier when rolling to damage enemy units during their next Turn (any rolls the unit makes of a natural 6 will still cause damage, however). Multiple castings of this spell, or combining it with Weakness, do not cause additional modifiers. Additionally, for each hit scored, roll a single D3 and total the results. This total is the amount of attacks to roll for damaging the target.	-	(2) for 25pts	(3) for 35pts	-
Scorched Earth	18"	Enemy	If one or more hits are successfully scored, during the following Turn any charges made by the target unit will be Hindered. In addition, the target unit loses the Strider and Pathfinder special rules for the duration of its next Turn.	-	(2) for 20pts	(3) for 30pts	-
Host Shadowbeast	12"	Friendly, Self, CC	May only target a friendly unit with the Individual special rule. For each hit scored, the target unit gains +1 attacks when attacking in Melee for the rest of the Turn. Multiple, subsequent castings from different sources are not cumulative.	-	(6) for 20pts	(8) for 30pts	(10) for 40pts

MAGICAL ARTEFACTS

Below are some new, and some replacement, Magical Artefacts to bolster and enhance your units. Where the name of an artefact is the same as a previous version, this is a complete replacement for the rules for that artefact (including the points cost). For example, the Darklord's Onyx Ring artefact presented here is a complete replacement for the one in the main rulebook.

COMMON ARTEFACTS

Banner of Eternal Darkness   10 pts

The unit gains the *Mindthirst* special rule.

Skirmisher's Boots   10 pts

Troops only. The unit gains the *Nimble* special rule.

Orb of Towering Presence   [10/15] pts

May not be taken by units with the *Individual* or *Fly* special rules. Increase the unit's Unit Strength by one, to a maximum of four.

Helm of the Drunken Ram   [15/20] pts

The unit gains the *Thunderous Charge* (+1) special rule, but may not benefit from the *Strider* and *Pathfinder* special rules when issued a Charge order.

Diadem of Dragonkind   30 pts

The unit gains the Fireball (8) spell, or if the unit already has a Fireball spell, its value is increased by 6.

HEROIC ARTEFACTS

Ej Periscope   5 pts

Infantry and Heavy Infantry only. This unit increases its Height by 1 when it draws Line of Sight.

Amulet of the Fireheart   10 pts

Once per game, immediately after casting a spell, the unit may cast a second, different, spell.

The unit cannot use this artefact to cast more than two spells in a single turn.

Darklord's Onyx Ring   10 pts

Individuals only. Once per game, the unit gains the

Regeneration (4+) special rule. This must be used the first time the unit has any damage on it at the beginning of the unit's Turn.

Gnome-Glass Shield   10 pts

Individuals only. The unit's Defence is increased by 2 to a maximum of 6. Immediately after the unit suffers damage for the first time (from any source) the Gnome-Glass Shield shatters and its Defence returns to normal for the rest of the game.

Torc of Dissonance   10 pts

Once per game, choose an enemy unit with a spellcaster tier within 12". Choose one of the spells known to that unit. During the enemy player's following Turn, the unit may not use the chosen spell.

Wingbane Cloak — 10 pts

The unit gains the *Ensnare* special rule against units with the *Fly* special rule. This artefact may not be given to units with the *Fly* special rule.

Axe of the Giant Slayer — 15 pts

Individuals only. The unit gains the *Slayer* (D3) special rule.

Crown of the Wizard King — 15 pts

The unit gains an additional 6" range on all of its spells that target Friendly units.

Scythe of the Harvester — 15 pts

Individuals only. The unit gains the *Rampage* (D3) special rule.

Talisman of Silence — 15 pts

The unit gains the Mindfog (2) spell.

Wand of Borrowed Time — 15 pts

Immediately after casting a spell, the unit may cast a different spell, but must choose a different target unit. After resolving the second spell casting, this unit may not cast any spells during its following Turn.

Banner of Abbetshire — 20 pts

The unit gains *Aura (Spellward)* special rule.

Tome of Darkness — 20 pts

The unit gains the Surge (5) spell, or if the unit already has a Surge spell, its value is increased by 3.

Zephyr Crown — 20 pts

The unit gains the Windblast (5) spell, or if the unit already has a Windblast spell, its value is increased by 3.

Shroud of the Saint — 25 pts

The unit gains the Heal (3) spell, or if the unit already has a Heal spell, its value is increased by 2.

The Boomstick — 25 pts

The unit gains the Lighting Bolt (3) spell, or if the unit already has a Lightning Bolt spell, its value is increased by 2.

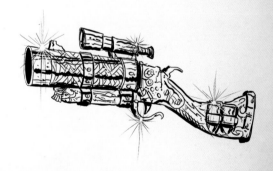

2022 ARMY CHANGES

On the pages that follow, you will find the units that have been adjusted following results from events and general shifts in the game meta, as well as some new units and Formations for your armies. Changed units replace those previously printed and all previous changes (e.g. in the last Clash of Kings book and in online errata) have been incorporated here as a single source.

BASILEANS

Sisterhood Scouts

Amend Unit Strength to 1/3 and amend attacks to 10/12 for Troops and Regiments respectively.

Dictator

Amend points cost to 75. Add the following option:

- Iron Discipline [1] for +15 pts - Unless Disordered, at the start of each of your Ranged phases, you may select a single Friendly Core unit with the **Human** keyword within 12" of the Dictator and Line of Sight. This unit immediately suffers D3 points of damage and gains Vicious (Melee) and Inspiring (Self) until the start of their following Turn. No Nerve tests are required for damage caused in this way.

Elohi

This unit is no longer Irregular, but still cannot be taken as Allies. Add the following option:

- Celestial Fury: Lower Defence to 4+ and gain Crushing Strength (2) for free.

Elohi, Ur-Elohi, and Jullius, Dragon of Heaven.

Add the following unique special rule:

Divine Fervour: Friendly Core units with the **Human** keyword, while Engaged with the same enemy unit as a unit with Divine Fervour, have Elite (Melee).

Sisterhood Infantry

Amend points cost to 90/135/225 for the Troop, Regiment and Horde respectively.

Sisterhood Chariots.

This unit is no longer Irregular. Amend Melee value to 3+.

Abbess.

Gains the Individual special rule. Add the following option:

- Aura (Fury - **Sisterhood** only) for +15 pts.

High Paladin on Dragon

Amend Nerve value to 17/19 and gain the Headstrong special rule.

New Unit

Tollivar, the Seer [1]						Ht
Hero (Inf), Spellcaster (3)						2

Sp 5	Me 5+	Unit Size	US	Att	Ne	Pts
Ra -	De 4+	1	0	1	11/13	150

Special Rules

Individual, Inspiring, Iron Resolve

Celestial Visions: Tollivar adds 6" to the range of his Bane Chant & Bastion spells when targeting friendly core **Angelic** units.

Celestial Providence: After successfully casting Bastion, Tollivar may immediately cast another different spell against the same or different target.

Spells

Bane Chant (3), Bastion [1] (2), Fireball (10)

Keywords: Human

Formation

The Golden Panthers

The Golden Panthers have a kinship with their beasts that few other orders have managed. Sister and panther operating as one, they are able to weave through the densest forests that would dismount others. The bond has given their panthers a fierce sense of loyalty, fighting to the death to protect their masters.

- 2 Troops of Gur Panthers

- 2 Regiments of Panther Lancers (+15 pts per unit)

The Panther Lancers in this Formation gain the Pathfinder and Aura (Fury - **Beast** only) special rules.

Total Formation cost: +30 pts

DWARFS

Berserkers

Amend Nerve values to -/15 and -/18 for the Troop and Regiment respectively, both gain the Slayer (Melee – D6) special rule.

Steel Behemoth

Amend Speed to 5 and gain the Wild Charge (D3) special rule. Amend points cost to 245.

Amend the Golloch's Fury upgrade to read:

Upgrade to Golloch's Fury [1] - Gain Very Inspiring and Aura (Iron Resolve - **Dwarf** only) and exchange the unit's Flame Belcher for Golloch's Gun: 18", Att: 12, Piercing (2) for +50 pts.

Ironwatch Rifles and Ironwatch Crossbows

Amend Melee values to 4+ and Unit Strength to 1/3/4 for the Troops, Regiment and Horde respectively.

Battle Driller

Amend points cost to 75 and Brutal to Brutal (2).

Warsmith

Gains the Inspiring special rule. Amend Aura to Aura (Elite (Ranged) - **Warsmith** and **Ironwatch** only)

Stone Priest

Add the following option:

- Purchase Radiance of Life (**Dwarf** only) for 25pts, or free if it replaces Surge.

Garrek Heavyhand

Gains the Radiance of Life special rule.

Sharpshooters

The unit type should be Heavy Infantry.

Greater Earth Elemental

Amend Attacks to 12.

Flame Belcher

Replace with the following profile:

Flame Belcher War Engine							Ht 2
Sp 4	Me -	Unit Size	US	Att	Ne	Pts	
Ra 4+	De 5+	1	0	15	10/12	90	

Special Rules
Flame Belch: 14", Steady Aim, Shattering
Keywords: Dwarf, Flamesmith, Warsmith

New Unit

Faber Ironheart [1] Hero (Lrg Inf)							Ht 3
Sp 5	Me 3+	Unit Size	US	Att	Ne	Pts	
Ra 5+	De 6+	1	1	7	-/15	175	

Special Rules
Crushing Strength (2), Inspiring, Nimble, Wild Charge (D3)
Hand Cannon: 24", Piercing (2), Steady Aim
Keywords: Dwarf, Warsmith

Formation

The Royal Guard

As a dwarf warrior gains renown on the battlefield, and their beard grows long, they may be recruited into their Hold's Royal Guard. These elite veterans are equipped with the best equipment their hold can muster and provide the last line of defence in times of crisis, striking fear into the hearts of those who dare to challenge them.

- The Hammers of the King (Two Regiments of Bulwarkers) (+15 pts per unit)

- Anvils of the Mountain (One Horde of Ironclad) (+20 pts)

- The Lord's Bannerman (One Dwarf Army Standard Bearer) (+30 pts)

All units in this Formation increase their Melee value to 3+ and Increase their Waver and Rout Nerve values by +1.

The Lord's Bannerman gains the Very Inspiring and Aura (Elite (melee) - Infantry only) special rules. It may not purchase a magic artefact.

Total Formation cost: +80 pts

ELVES

Elven Archmage.

Amend spellcaster tier to 3.

- May take Surge (8) for +30 pts

Kindred Gladestalkers.

This unit is no longer Irregular. Amend Melee value to 3+, Unit Strength to 1/3 and Attacks to 10/12 for Troops and Regiments respectively.

Kindred Archers

Amend Ranged value to 4+ and Defence to 3+. Amend points cost to 105/140/245 for the Troop, Regiment and Horde respectively.

Stormwind Cavalry

Add the following option:

- Upgrade to Quicksilver Lancers [1] (Regiment only) - Gain Nimble and increase the the unit's Waver and Rout Nerve values by +1 for +25 pts.

Drakon Riders

This unit is no longer Irregular.

Therennian Seaguard

This unit's Bows attack gains the Steady Aim special rule. Amend points cost to 150/260 for the Regiment and Horde respectively.

Hunters of the Wild

Amend points cost to 90/140 points for the Troop and Regiment respectively.

Dragon Kindred Lord

Amend points cost to 305.

Lord on Drakon

Amend points cost to 160.

Tydarion Dragon Lord

Amend points cost to 335. Gains the Nimble special rule.

Argus Rodinar

Add the following unique special rule:

Master Strategist: As long as this unit is present and in play on the table, once per Turn the unit's player may re-roll a single dice that failed to either hit or damage with any Friendly Core unit, regardless of range and Line of Sight to Argus.

The text of the Altar of the Elements rule should read:

As long as this unit is present and in play on the table, at the start of each of your ranged phases you may select a single Friendly Core unit on the battlefield regardless of range or line of sight. The unit is granted the Inspiring special rule until the start of your next turn.

New Units

Kindred Warriors
Infantry

			Unit Size	US	Att	Ne	Pts	Ht
Sp 6	Me 4+		Troop (10)	1	10	10/12	80	2
Ra -	De 4+		Regiment (20)	3	12	14/16	120	
			Horde (40)	4	25	21/23	200	

Special Rules
Elite (Melee)
Keywords: Elf, Kindred

Drakon Hatchling Pack*
Swarm

			Unit Size	US	Att	Ne	Pts	Ht
Sp 7	Me 4+		Regiment (3)	1	12	10/12	115	2
Ra -	De 3+		Horde (6)	1	24	14/16	195	

Special Rules
Crushing Strength (1), Fly, Nimble.
Keywords: Draconic

King's Champion [1]
Hero (Inf)

		Ht 2

Sp 7	Me 3+	Unit Size	US	Att	Ne	Pts
Ra -	De 5+	1	1	7	14/16	145

Special Rules
Aura (Fury - **Kindred** only), Crushing Strength (1), Duelist, Elite (Melee), Individual, Mighty, Phalanx, Very Inspiring
Keywords: Elf, Kindred

Nimue Waydancer [1]
Hero (Inf), Spellcaster (1)

		Ht 2

Sp 6	Me 5+	Unit Size	US	Att	Ne	Pts
Ra -	De 4+	1	0	1	12/14	150

Special Rules
Cloak of Death, Individual, Inspiring, Stealthy
Wanderer of the Ways: Once per game, before Nimue Waydancer is given an order, she increases her Speed to 10 and gains the Fly special rule until the end of the turn. In the turn this ability is activated, Nimue Waydancer may still cast spells even if she was given an At The Double order.
Spells
Fireball (10), Heal (4), Surge (4), Wind Blast (5)
Keywords: Elf, Verdant

Formation

Kal'ar's Hunters

Admiral Kal'ar is a seasoned campaigner in the elven navy, and likes to direct the ships under his command while riding a mighty drakon, accompanied by a loyal, yet mysterious group of Drakon Riders known only as the Swirling Tempests.

- Kal'ar Drakonkin (One Drakon Rider Lord) (+10 pts)

- The Swirling Tempests (Two Drakon Rider Regiments) (+15 pts per unit)

All units in this Formation gain the Spellward special rule. Kal'ar gains the Rampage (Melee - D3) special rule. The Swirling Tempests gain the Nimble special rule.

Total Formation cost: +40 pts

NORTHERN ALLIANCE

Elf Clansmen

Amend Ranged value to 4+, Defence to 3+ and points cost to 105/140 for the Troop and Regiment respectively.

Human Clansmen

Amend Defence to 4 and points cost to 80/120/200. Add the following options:

- Upgrade to Norj-Bik Clansmen, increasing Defence to 5+ for +10/15/25pts

- Exchange shields for two-handed weapons, lowering Defence to 3+ and gaining Crushing Strength (2) for [0] pts

Clarion

Amend Melee value to 3+, Attacks to 5 and points cost to 115 points.

Frost Giant

Gains the Slayer (Melee - D6) special rule.

Hrimm, the Legendary Giant

Gains the Slayer (Melee - D6) special rule.

Ice Kin Hunters

This unit is no longer Irregular. Amend Melee value to 3+, Unit Strength to 1/3 and Attacks to 10/12 for the Troop and Regiment respectively.

Pack Hunters

This unit is no longer Irregular.

Ice Elementals

Remove Spellcaster 0. Add Ra 4+ to the unit's profile.

Replace Icy Breath (Att) with Ice Shards: Ranged: 10", Piercing (1), Steady Aim

Amend the Frostbite unique special rule to: "If one or more points of damage are scored with this unit's Ice Shards attack, the target enemy unit is given the Frozen special rule."

Lord

Amend Attacks to 6. Add the following option:

- Mount on a Horse, losing Wild Charge (1) but increasing Speed to 8 and changing to Hero (Cav - Height: 3) for +35 pts

Lord on Chimera

Amend points cost to 310.

New Unit

Serakina, the Ice Queen [1]						Ht 2
Hero (Inf), Spellcaster (2)						

Sp 6	Me 5+	Unit Size	US	Att	Ne	Pts
Ra -	De 4+	1	0	1	11/13	130

Special Rules

Ensnare, Individual, Very Inspiring, Radiance of Life (**Frostbound** only)

Frozen Winds: If one or more hits are scored with Serakina's Wind Blast spell, the target enemy unit is given the Frozen special rule for the duration of its next Turn.

Spells

Surge (8), Wind Blast (6)

Keywords: Frostbound

Formation

Orlaf's Raiders

Orlaf the Barbarian has gained considerable recognition throughout the frozen lands under the control of the Northern Alliance, so much so that Clansmen with an appetite for war have begun to flock to his side. When taking to the battlefield alongside Orlaf, these raiders are driven on to fight harder, hoping to seek recognition from the great berserker himself.

- Two human Clansmen Regiments (must swap shields for 2-handed weapons) (+10 pts each)

- Orlaf the Barbarian (+25 pts)

All units in this Formation gain keyword: **Berserker**. The Clansmen regiments gain the Vicious (Melee) special rule. Orlaf gains the Inspiring and Aura (Slayer (Melee - D3) - **Berserker** only) special rules.

Total Formation cost: +45 pts

FORCES OF NATURE

Add the **Elemental** keyword to the following units: Air Elementals, Druid, Earth Elementals, Fire Elementals, Forest Shamblers, Gladewalker Druid, Greater Air Elemental, Greater Earth Elemental, Greater Fire Elemental, Greater Water Elemental and Water Elementals.

Greater Air elemental

Gains the Crushing Strength (1) special rule.

Naiad Heartpiercers

This unit is no longer Irregular.

Unicorn

Amend the cost of Lightning Bolt (5) to +35 points.

Scorchwings

Amend Defence value to 4+ and Attacks to 7/14 for the Regiment and Horde respectively.

Greater Fire Elemental

Amend Melee value to 3+.

Greater Water Elemental

Amend Attacks to 9 and gain the Regeneration (4+) special rule.

Tree Herder

Add the following option:

- Upgrade to The Wiltfather [1] - Losing Radiance of Life, Increasing Attacks to 10, Nerve to -/19 and gaining Aura (Vicious - Verdant Only) & Cloak of Death for +40 points. This upgrade cannot be taken in addition to a magical artefact.

Avatar of the Green Lady

Amend points cost to 150. Gains the Pathfinder special rule.

Pegasus

Gains the Nimble special rule.

Gladewalker Druid

Add the following unique special rule:

Nature in Balance: While within 6" of another friendly Core Elemental unit, this unit can reroll all to-hit rolls of a natural, unmodified 1 with Fireball, Blizzard, Heal, Hex, and Surge spells.

Add the following upgrade:

- Ring of Harmony [1]: Once per Turn, after casting a spell targeting a Friendly Core Elemental unit, this unit may immediately target a different Friendly Core Elemental unit with the same or a different spell, for 25pts.

Centaur Bray Striders

Add a Horde option as follows:

Unit Size	US	Att	Ne	Pts
Horde (20)	4	24	21/23	270

Profile Replacement

The following profile replaces Naiad Wyrmriders for this army.

Riverbourne Naiad Wyrmriders

Large Cavalry

Sp	Me	Unit Size	US	Att	Ne	Pts	Ht
7	3+	Regiment (3)	2	9	12/14	140	4
Ra	De	Horde (6)	3	18	15/17	235	
-	4+						

Special Rules
Crushing Strength (1), Pathfinder, Regeneration (4+), Thunderous Charge (2)

Keywords: Naga, Naiad

New Unit

Kapoka, the Hidden Saviour [1]

Hero (Hv Inf), Spellcaster (2)

Sp	Me	Unit Size	US	Att	Ne	Pts	Ht
5	-	1	0	-	12/14	145	2
Ra	De						
-	4+						

Special Rules
Aura (Phalanx - **Verdant** only), Individual, Inspiring, Pathfinder, Scout, Stealthy

Spells
Heal (4), Weakness (3)

Keywords: Verdant

Formation

Nature's Wrath

When the elemental forces of water and air combine, it usually only results in storms or rain showers. However, sometimes this natural phenomenon is manipulated by the Druids of the Green Lady and they are able to coax the elementals within the maelstrom to fight at their side.

- 2 Air Elemental hordes (+10 pts each)
- 1 Greater Air Elemental (+20 pts)

All units in this Formation gain the keyword: **Waterbound** and the Regeneration (5+) special rule.

The Greater Air Elemental gains the Aura (Brutal - **Airbound** & **Waterbound** only) special rule.

Total Formation cost: +40 pts

Ogres

Army Construction. For each Ogre Warrior regiment in the army, you can also include one of the following units: Hero, Monster, Titan, War Engine.

Ogre Warriors

Amend Regiment Nerve to 12/14.

Ogre Sergeant

Gains the Elite and Steady Aim special rules.

Ogre Boomer Chariots

Gains the Aura (Stealthy) special rule.

Red Goblin Scouts*

Increase this unit's nerve to 10/12, and 13/15 for the troop and regiment respectively.

Ogre Hunters

Gains the Slayer (Melee - D3) special rule.

Giant

Gains the Slayer (Melee - D6) special rule.

Red Goblin Slasher

Amend Attacks to 10. Add the following option:

• Aura (Fury - **Goblin** only) [1] for 15pts

Mammoth

Gains the Rampage (Melee - D6) special rule.

Add the following option:

• Upgrade to The Big Deal [1] - Increasing to Brutal (2) and gain both the Very Inspiring special rule, as well as the **Call to Greatness** unique special rule (see below) for +30 pts.

Call to Greatness. As long as this unit is present and in play on the table, at the start of each of your Melee phases you may select a single friendly Core unit with the Ogre keyword within 12" regardless of range or Line of Sight. The selected unit is granted the Brutal (+1) special rule until the start of your next Turn.

Ogre Warlock

Add "or Large Infantry Legion" to the Ogre Warlock rule of friendly units within 6".

Formation
Hell on Wheels

Champion of many brutal ogre chariot racing competitions, Rugamok is often paid handsomely by other ogre warlords to take his charioteering skills to the battlefield. Rugamok allows younger aspiring charioteers to fight alongside him, and even provides them with guidance and tutelage, on the condition that they never race against him, and that they provide him with a slice of their winnings.

• One Warlord on Chariot (+15 pts)

• Two Ogre Chariot Regiments (+5 pts per unit)

The Warlord on Chariot gains the Rallying (1 - Chariot only) special rule. Each unit in this Formation gains the Rampage (D3) special rule.

Total Formation cost: +25 pts

New Units

Crocodog Wrangler
Monster (Cav)

Ht	
2	

Sp	Me	Unit Size	US	Att	Ne	Pts
6	3+	1	0	7	11/13	110

Ra	De
-	4+

Special Rules
Crushing Strength (1), Duelist, Individual, Vicious (melee), Wild Charge (D3+1).
Through the Legs: Friendly Core units with the **Ogre** keyword do not block Line of Sight and can be charged through by the Crocodog Wrangler, as long as it ends its movement clear.
Keywords: Beast, Crocodog, Goblin

Nomagarok [1]
Hero (Lrg Inf) Spellcaster (2)

Ht	
3	

Sp	Me	Unit Size	US	Att	Ne	Pts
6	4+	1	1	5	12/14	140

Ra	De
-	5+

Special Rules
Brutal, Crushing Strength (1), Inspiring, Nimble
Ogre Warlock: For each friendly core Large Infantry Regiment, Large Infantry Horde or Large Infantry Legion within 6", increase the amount of dice rolled with Bane Chant, Heal and Lightning Bolt by 1 to a maximum bonus of +3.
Bloodlust: Any friendly core unit hit with Nomagarok's Heal spell gains Vicious (Melee) for the remainder of the Turn.
Spells
Bane Chant (3), Heal (4), Lightning Bolt (4)
Keywords: Berserker, Ogre, Warlock

TRIDENT REALM OF NERITICA

Naiad Heartpiercers

This unit is no longer Irregular.

Thuul

Gains the Wild Charge (D3) special rule.

Thuul Mythican

Gains the Wild Charge (D3) special rule.

Leviathan Bane

Amend points cost to 95 points and Leviathan Bolts attack to Piercing (2).

Add the following option:

• Increase Leviathan Bolts to Piercing (3) for 10pts.

Amend the Harpoon rule to the following:

After dealing damage with this unit's Leviathan Bolts attack, you may choose to immediately move the enemy unit (n) inches as if Enthral had been cast successfully on the target unit, where (n) is the amount of damage inflicted with the Leviathan Bolts attack.

Depth Horrors

Amend Nerve value to 13/15 for the Regiment and 16/18 for the Horde, both gain the Fury special rule.

Depth Horror Eternal

Amend nerve to 14/16 and gain the Fury special rule.

Coral Giant

Amend attacks to D6+8 and gain the Slayer (Melee - D6) special rule.

Kraken

Add the Rampage (Melee - D3) special rule.

Riverguard Sentinel

This unit's Javelin gains Piercing (1).

Naiad Centurion

Gains the Ensnare special rule.

Add the following option:

• Trident of the Drowned Sea [1] for 25pts: Range 12", Piercing (1). This unit gains Ra 3+. Units that suffer a point of damage from the Trident of the Drowned Sea are Disordered during their next turn.

Siren

Add the following special rule:

Siren's Call: This unit's Enthral spell range is increased to 24". Also, if one or more hits are scored, make a Nerve test for the target at the end of the Ranged phase as though damage had been caused.

Greater Water Elemental

Increase this unit's attacks to 9 and its Regeneration to (4+).

Placoderms

Amend Troop Nerve to 10/12.

Profile Replacements

Riverguard Infantry					Ht 2
Sp 7	Me 4+	**Unit Size**	**US**	**Att**	**Ne**	**Pts**
Ra 5+	De 3+	Troop (10)	1	10	9/11	120
		Regiment (20)	2	12	13/15	160

Special Rules
Ensnare, Fly, Nimble, Pathfinder
Javelins: 12", Piercing (1), Steady Aim
Keywords: Amphibian, Tracker

The following profile replaces Naiad Wyrmriders for this army.

Oceanborne Naiad Wyrmriders
Large Cavalry

Sp	Me	Unit Size	US	Att	Ne	Pts
8	3+	Regiment (3)	2	9	13/15	155
Ra	De	Horde (6)	3	18	16/18	255
-	4+					

Ht 4

Special Rules
Crushing Strength (1), Nimble, Pathfinder, Regeneration (4+)
Keywords: Naga, Naiad

New Unit

Kyroqsh, the Hunter in the Deep [1]
Hero (Inf), Spellcaster (1)

Sp	Me	Unit Size	US	Att	Ne	Pts
7	3+	1	0	5	12/14	140
Ra	De					
-	4+					

Ht 2

Special Rules
Crushing Strength (1), Ensnare, Individual, Inspiring, Scout, Stealthy, Wild Charge (D3)
Hunter in the Deep: Kyroqsh gains Vicious (Melee) and has Double attacks vs Large Cavalry, Monsters and Titans only.
Spells
Lightning Bolt (3)
Keywords: Cephalopod

Formation

The Hidden Ones

Ineesha has had an affinity for land that few Thuul care for. Her wanderlust has taken her and her followers up rivers and onto lands far from any sea. Their travels have given them an unparalleled knowledge of fieldcraft among their kind. While Ineesha is not violent by nature, she has learned that in the dangerous world of Pannithor, those who don't strike hard are often left a few tentacles short.

- The Hidden Ones (two regiments of Thuul) (+10 pts per unit)

- Ineesha (One Thuul Mythican) (+10 pts)

All units in this Formation gain the Pathfinder special rule. The Thuul Mythican gains the Aura (Thunderous Charge (1) - **Cephalopod** only) special rule.

Total Formation cost: +30 pts

ABYSSAL DWARFS

Abyssal Halfbreeds

Gains the Fury special rule.

Taskmaster on Chariot

Amend Melee value to 3+. Gains the Rallying (1 - **Slave** only) special rule and loses the option to purchase Rallying (1 - **Slave** only).

Hellfane

Amend points cost to 265 and gain the Rampage (D6) special rule.

Blacksouls.

Add the following option:

- Fiery Bulwark [1] for 10pts. This unit gains the Iron Resolve special rule. When this unit's Iron Resolve is used, it can regain D3 points of damage previously suffered, instead of one.

Angkor Heavy Mortar

Amend to Piercing (2).

Hexcaster

The unit's Weakness option should read: "Weakness (3) for +20 points". There is no longer a free replacement option.

Iron Caster

Amend points cost to 90. Remove "Heal (3- Hellforged only)". Add the option: Heal (3) for +20 points.

Supreme Iron Caster on Great Winged Halfbreed

Amend points cost to 270. Replace the option for Heal (4 - **Hellforged** only) with Heal (4) for +20 pts.

Greater Obsidian Golem

Amend Attacks to 12.

Ba'su'su the Vile

Add the following option:

A single troop of Gargoyles* in this army can be upgraded to be **Ba'su'su's Vile Brood*** [1] - Which gain the **Abomination** Keyword, Crushing Strength (1) special rule and Increase their Waver and Rout Nerve values by +2 for +25 pts.

Formation

The Damned of Yaygar

Bound for all eternity to wage war in the name of their master, Yaygar Jagmaw, The souls of the Damned writhe and flail in a raging fire deep within the husks of their former bodies, barely held together inside their ancient and battleworn armour. The hellish inferno is a blessing and a curse – for it fuels their strikes with Abyssal hate, but weakens their defences in equal measure. Such is the price of endless servitude.

- 2 Regiments of Immortal Guard

- 1 Infernox (+35 pts)

The Immortal Guard units in this formation lower their Defence to 4+ and gain Crushing Strength (1). The Infernox gains Inspiring, and Aura (Elite (Melee - Infantry only)).

Total Formation cost: +35 pts

New Units

Dravak Dalkan [1]

Hero (Inf), Spellcaster (2)

							Ht
							2

Sp	Me	Unit Size	US	Att	Ne	Pts
4	4+	1	0	2	12/14	155
Ra	De					
-	5+					

Special Rules

Crushing Strength (1), Individual, Inspiring

Possession: Unless Infernok is Engaged or Disordered, Dravak Dalkan may use Infernok's Line of Sight to cast spells. When doing so, measure range from Infernok's leader point instead of Dravak Dalkan's.

Spells

Fireball (12), Heal (3), Surge (12)

Keywords: Dwarf, Hellforged

Infernok [1]

Titan

							Ht
							6

Sp	Me	Unit Size	US	Att	Ne	Pts
6	4+	1	1	12	-/19	255
Ra	De					
-	6+					

Special Rules

Brutal (1), Crushing Strength (4), Shambling, Strider, Vicious (Melee)

Bound Soul: As long as a friendly core Dravak Dalkan is alive and in play, Infernok has the Inspiring (Self) special rule.

Keywords: Hellforged

EMPIRE OF DUST

Apaphys, Champion of Death [1]

Amend points cost to 350.

Reanimated Behemoth

Amend Melee value to 3+, gains the Slayer (Melee - D6) special rule.

Revenant on Undead Great Burrowing Wyrm

Amend points cost to 200.

Revenant Cavalry

Amend points cost to 115/180 for the Troop and Regiment respectively.

Revenant Champion

This unit now has Spellcaster 0.

Add the following option:

- May take Surge (5) for 10 pts.

Skeleton Warriors

Add the following option:

- Exchange shields for two-handed weapons, lowering Defence to 3+ and gaining Crushing Strength (1) for [+5/5/10] pts.

Ahmunite Pharaoh on Royal Chariot

Amend the cost of Surge (8) to 15 points.

Add the following option:

Upgrade to Rahs The Undying [1] - Replacing Inspiring with Very Inspiring and Increasing the unit's Rout value by +1. The unit also gains the Restore Ancient Glory unique special rule (see below) for +50 pts:

Restore Ancient Glory: While attacking the same enemy unit as Rahs the Undying in Melee, Core friendly units with the Skeleton keyword may replace their own Melee value with Rahs' Melee value - apply any subsequent modifiers as normal. Cannot be taken with magical artefact.

Ahmunite Pharaoh

Amend the **The Eternal Guard [1]** option to: Aura (Elite (Melee – **Mummy** only)).

Revenant King on Undead Great Flying Wyrm

Amend Nerve value to -/18 and points cost to 265.

Cursed High Priest

Replace the Drain Life spell option with: Drain Life (6) for 30 points.

Replace the Reanimator unique special rule with: "For each other Friendly Core Skeleton unit within 6", you may re-roll one die that failed to hit with Drain Life, Fireball, Heal, Hex, Surge, Weakness and Wind Blast up to a maximum of two re-rolls."

Soul Snare

This unit now has Spellcaster: 1

Monolith

The text of the Monolith rule should read:

As long as this unit is alive and in play on the table, at the start of each of your ranged phases you may immediately cast Surge (8) on a single Friendly Core unit anywhere within 24" of this unit regardless of line of sight.

Note: The Monolith cannot be disordered and its Base size cannot be increased beyond 75x75mm.

Profile Replacement

Revenant Chariots					Ht 3
Chariot					

		Unit Size	US	Att	Ne	Pts
Sp 8	**Me** 4+	Troop (2)	1	8	-/14	110
		Regiment (3)	2	12	-/16	140
Ra 5+	**De** 4+	Horde (4)	3	16	-/18	175
		Legion (6)	4	20	-/21	205

Special Rules
Brutal, Lifeleech (1), Shambling, Thunderous Charge (2)
Options
May purchase Cursebows gaining Ra5+ and the following ranged attack:
Cursebows: Range 18", Att: [4/6/8/10], Shattering, Steady Aim for [+5/5/10/15] points
Keywords: Revenant, Skeleton

New Units

Sandborne Wyrm Riders
Large Cavalry

Sp	Me	Unit Size	US	Att	Ne	Pts
7	4+	Regiment (3)	2	12	12/14	135
Ra	De	Horde (6)	3	24	15/17	225
-	5+					

Special Rules
Crushing Strength (1), Lifeleech (1), Pathfinder
Keywords: Naga, Revenant, Skeleton

Sebekh-Rei the Accursed [1]
Hero (Inf), Spellcaster (3)

Sp	Me	Unit Size	US	Att	Ne	Pts
5	5+	1	0	1	-/13	155
Ra	De					
-	4+					

Special Rules
Individual, Very Inspiring
Glory of the Accursed: For each other Friendly Core Skeleton unit within 6", you may re-roll one die that failed to hit with Heal, and Surge, up to a maximum of two re-rolls..
Glory for the Mighty Dead: After casting Heal on a friendly core unit, this unit may immediately cast Surge against the same target.
Spells
Heal (5), Surge (8)
Keywords: Accursed, Skeletal

Formation

The Bone Shakers

Legends tell of an Ahmunite High-King so vain that he refused to have any of his soldiers tread upon the earth. Instead, all of them were mounted upon a host of chariots that stretched as far as the eye could see. Many a foe came to fear the earth-shaking charge and all too many were run down by the glorious legion and its stalwart champions.

- 2 Revenant Chariot regiments (+10 pts per unit)
- 1 Revenant Chariot Legion (+15 pts)
- 1 Revenant Champion (+10 pts)

The Revenant Champion in this formation must purchase a mount. The Revenant Champion and Revenant Chariot Regiments in this formation gain the Rampage (D3 - melee) special rule. The Revenant Chariot Legion in this formation gains the Rampage (D6 - melee) special rule.

Total Formation cost: +45 pts

FORCES OF THE ABYSS

Archfiend of the Abyss

Amend Nerve to 17/19 and points cost to 305.

Chroneas

Amend Melee value to 3+ and points cost to 225 points. Add the following unique special rule:

Temporal Ruptures: For each point of damage the Chroneas causes in Melee, you may remove a point of damage from a single Core friendly unit within 6" of the Chroneas (other than the Chroneas itself) to a maximum of three per Turn.

The Well of Souls

Amend points cost to 290 and increase Lifeleech to 5 - note this is an exception to the usual limit of Lifeleech 3.

Flamebearers

This unit is no longer Irregular.

Molochs

Amend the Despoiler Champion upgrade to read: May be upgraded with a Despoiler Champion gaining the Vicious (Melee) and Brutal special rules for [+15/+20] points.

Lower Abyssals

Amend the option to exchange their shields to read: "Exchange shields for two-handed weapons, lowering Defence to 3+ and gaining Crushing Strength (1) for free".

Tortured Souls

Gains the Thunderous Charge (1) special rule.

Manifestation of Ba'el

Gains the Nimble special rule.

Ba'su'su the Vile

Add the following option:

• A single troop of Gargoyles* in this army can be upgraded to be **Ba'su'su's Vile Brood* [1]** - Which gain the **Abomination** Keyword, Crushing Strength (1) special rule and Increase their Waver and Rout Nerve values by +2 for +25 pts.

New Units

The Oathbreakers [1]
Infantry

		Unit Size	US	Att	Ne	Pts	Ht
Sp 5	Me 3+	Regiment (20)	3	12	-/17	175	2
Ra -	De 4+						

Special Rules
Crushing Strength (1), Rallying (1 – Infantry only), Regeneration (5+), Vicious (Melee – Heroes only)
Keywords: Abyssal, Oathbreaker

Zaz'u'szu The Betrayer [1]
Hero (Lrg Inf), Spellcaster: 2

		Unit Size	US	Att	Ne	Pts	Ht
Sp 6	Me 4+	1	1	5	12/14	115	3
Ra -	De 4+						

Special Rules
Fury, Nimble, Inspiring, Regeneration (5+)
Betrayal: At the start of each of his shooting phases, Zaz'u'szu may select a single friendly Core unit within 6" to be his sacrifice. If he does so, Zaz'u'szu may increase the number of dice used to cast his Lighting Bolt or Bane Chant spells by up to 4. For each hit scored with Zaz'u'szu's spells this turn, the sacrificial unit suffers a point of damage. No Nerve tests are required for damage caused in this way.
Spells
Lightning Bolt (4,) Bane Chant (2)
Keywords: Abyssal, Oathbreaker

Formation

Kah'za'ah's Torment

While many Despoilers lead the hulking Molochs into battle, Kah'za'ah is forced to oversee the pitiful ranks of the Lower Abyssals. This unenviable task was set for him as punishment for a discretion committed so long ago, even Kah'za'ah cannot remember its details. Bitter and resentful of his task, Kah'za'ah is a cruel and unyielding taskmaster and defeat on the battlefield often comes as a welcome reprieve for those under his command.

- Kah'za'ah's Maggots (One regiment, and one horde of Lower Abyssals) (+10 pts per unit)

- Kah'za'ah the Putrid (One Despoiler Champion) (+25 pts)

Kah'za'ah gains both the Inspiring and Aura (Lifeleech (+2) - Infantry only) special rules. Whenever a unit of Kah'za'ah's Maggots suffer a Rout result, all units in base contact with that unit suffer D3+1 hits with Piercing (1) and gain the Frozen special rule. No Nerve tests are required for damage caused in this way.

Total Formation cost: +45 pts

GOBLINS

Fleabag Riders

Amend Nerve to 10/12, 13/15 and 20/22 for the Troop, Regiment and Horde respectively.

Goblin Slasher

Amend Attacks to 10.

Add the following option:

- Aura (Rampage (Melee - D3) - **Beast** only) for 15pts

Giant

Gains the Slayer (Melee - D6) special rule.

Trolls

Add the following option:

- **Upgrade with Det' Packs [1] (Horde only)** - When this unit suffers a Rout result, all units, both Friendly and Enemy within 6" of it suffer D6+1 hits at Piercing (1). These hits are resolved by the player that Routed the unit with the Det' Packs. Roll once and apply the number of hits to all units within range. No Nerve tests are required for damage caused in this way.

Goblin King

Add the following option:

- **Upgrade to Groany Snark [1]** - Increasing speed to 10 and gain the Fly, Thunderous Charge (2) and Blast (D3) special rules as well as the Mini-Winggit Flight suit unique special rule (see below) for +30 pts. This unique upgrade cannot be taken in addition to a magical artefact or a mount.

Mini-Winggit Flight Suit

Before being given an order in the movement phase other than Halt, Change Facing or Counter Charge, roll a D6. On a result of a 1 the flight suit malfunctions in spectacular fashion. All units, both Friendly and Enemy within 6" of it take a point of damage, including this unit. No Nerve tests are required for damage taken in this way.

Profile Replacement

Winggit								Ht 3
Monster								

Sp 10	Me 5+	Unit Size	US	Att	Ne	Pts
Ra -	De 4+	1	1	1	11/13	120

Special Rules

Fly, Nimble

You may select one of the following options for free:

- **Ramming Speed!:** Increase Nerve to 13/15, attacks to 5 and Melee value to 4+. Gain the Thunderous Charge (1) and Vicious (Melee) special rules.
- **Bombs Away!:** Gain RA 4+ and the Eye in the Sky special rule (see below) and the following ranged attack:
  Firebombs: 12", Attack: 3, Blast (D3), Piercing (1), Steady Aim, Vicious (Ranged). Ignore Cover special rule.

Eye in the Sky: At the start of each of your Ranged phases you can immediately target and "mark" an Enemy unit anywhere within 24" of this unit regardless of Line of Sight. For the remainder of the Turn, all friendly Core units with the Lobber keyword, while targeting the marked enemy unit, have the Elite (Ranged) special rule. This special rule may not be used while the Winggit is Disordered.

Keywords: Gizmo, Goblin

New Units

Grogger's Lugg Lads [1]

Infantry

Ht 2

Sp 5	Me 4+	Unit Size	US	Att	Ne	Pts
Ra -	De 4+	Horde (40)	4	30	-/22	245

Special Rules
Brutal, Crushing Strength (1), Wild Charge (D3)
Keywords: Berserker, Goblin, Mawpup Cages

Grupp Longnail [1]

Hero (Inf), Spellcaster (1)

Ht 2

Sp 6	Me 3+	Unit Size	US	Att	Ne	Pts
Ra -	De 4+	1	0	4	-/12	90

Special Rules
Blast (D3), Crushing Strength (1), Duelist, Ensnare, Individual
FULG'UR!: When attacking in melee, if one or more hits are scored, the target unit has a -1 modifier when rolling to damage enemy units during their next Turn (any rolls the unit makes of natural six will still cause damage, however). This effect only applies once and does not work in conjunction with the Weakness spell.
Keywords: Gizmo, Goblin

Formation

Gorp's Explodo'matic Bangstiks

Gorp has always had a love for all things that go boom! With little thought for the safety of his fellow goblins, Gorp is constantly searching to find the perfect balance between the biggest bang possible, and not blowing himself, or others to smithereens in the process. He hasn't found that balance yet, but there are always more goblins ready to take up a Bangstik and continue his experiments.

- Gorp (One King on Fleabag) (+20 pts)
- The Bangstiks (Two Regiments of Fleabag Riders) (+10 pts per unit)

Gorp gains the Aura (Elite (Melee - Cavalry with the **Goblin** keyword only)) special rule. The Bangstiks units increase their Thunderous Charge to (2).

Whenever a unit in this Formation rolls a natural unmodified 6 to hit in Melee, resolve that hit with the Blast (2) special rule. In addition, for each 6 rolled the attacking unit receives a point of damage as the Bangstik backfires on the unlucky goblin wielding it. No Nerve tests are taken for damage caused in this way.

Total Formation cost: +40 pts

NIGHTSTALKERS

Bloodworms

Gains the Fury special rule and amend Nerve to 12/15, 19/22, and 25/28 for the Regiment, Horde, and Legion respectively.

Portal of Despair.

Add the following option:

- Gain Radiance of Life for 35 points

The text of the Visions of the Void rules should read:

As long as this unit is present and in play on the table, at the start of each of your Ranged phases you may select a single Friendly Core unit on the battlefield regardless of range or line of sight. The selected unit is granted the Inspiring special rule until the start of your next turn.

Note: Base size cannot be increased beyond 75x75mm.

Shadowhulk

Gains the Slayer (Melee - D3) special rule.

Banshee

Add the following option:

- Resonant Chorus [1] - Once per turn, after casting its Windblast or Enthral spell, the Banshee may immediately cast the same spell again on a different target within 6" of the original target (following all the usual target selection rules) for 25pts.

Reaper Souldrinker

Amend points cost to 80.

Doppelgangers

The text of the Doppelgangers rule should read:

When this unit attacks an enemy unit in melee, it may opt to use the Enemy's profile for its melee attacks instead of its own. If it does so then it uses the Enemy unit's Melee stat, Attacks stat and Crushing Strength value for that turn instead of its own. Any magical artefacts the Enemy unit has are ignored. The Doppelgangers themselves may still use a magic artefact as normal if they have one. Apply any bonuses and penalties granted by magic artefacts, spells, terrain or other sources after the decision on which stats to use.

Soulflayers

Amend attacks to 12.

Shadowhounds

Amend Speed to 10.

Butchers

Amend Nerve values to 13/15 and 16/18 for the Regiment and Horde respectively, both gain the Fury special rule.

Profile Replacement

Horror Riftweavers		Ht 2
Monster		

Sp 6	Me 3+	Unit Size	US	Att	Ne	Pts
Ra -	De 3+	1	1	D6+6	11/13	110

Special Rules
Aura (Spellward), Crushing Strength (1), Dread, Nimble, Mindthirst, Stealthy
Keywords: Horror, Nightmare

New Unit

Esenyshra, the Wailing Shadow [1]		Ht 2
Hero (Inf), Spellcaster (2)		

Sp 10	Me 3+	Unit Size	US	Att	Ne	Pts
Ra -	De 5+	1	0	5	-/13	160

Special Rules
Crushing Strength (3), Dread, Fly, Individual, Mighty, Mindthirst, Stealthy, Strider
Beguilement: If Esenyshra's Enthral spell causes enough hits that an enemy unit would be able to move into contact with Esenyshra herself, the normal 1" stopping restriction is lifted. After contact is made, Esenyshra may immediately charge and align against the enemy facing that was moved into contact with her. However, the charged unit will not take any Nerve tests for any damage it might have taken in the previous Ranged phase.
Spells
Enthral (7)
Keywords: Phantasm

Formation

Beaststalker Doomhounds

Lurking in the darkest corner of the Etheric Plane, the Beastseeker Doomhounds have developed a taste for the flesh of some of the larger beasts that roam Pannithor. Frothing at the mouth at the mere sight of a Giant, Kraken or Slasher, these hounds will attack their prey with an unparalleled ferocity and hunger.

- Doomhounds (three troops of Shadowhounds) (+5 pts per unit)

All units in the Formation gain the Slayer (Melee - D6) special rule.

Total Formation cost: +15 pts

ORCS

Add the following units from the Riftforged Orcs theme list. Reborn Legionaries*

Giant

Gains the Slayer (Melee - D6) special rule.

Godspeaker

Amend the Tribal Magic unique special rule to:

For each friendly Core Regiment, Horde or Legion with the **Orc** or **Troll** keyword within 6" of this unit, increase the amount of dice rolled with Bane Chant, Drain Life, Fireball, Heal and Hex by one, to a maximum bonus of three.

War Drum

Replace the options with:

- Upgrade the unit with Dread for +15 pts.

- Mount on a War Wagon, increasing Speed to 8, gaining Nimble and changing to Monster (Cht - Height: 3) for +30 pts.

Morax Mansplitter

Gains the Inspiring special rule.

Skulk Raider Chariots

This unit is no longer Irregular. Amend Nerve to 11/13 and 13/15 for the Troop and Regiment respectively.

Skulks

Gains the Steady Aim special rule.

Add the following option:

- Upgrade to Skulk Raiders - Gain Pathfinder and increase Melee value to 4+ for [+15/20] pts.

Skulk Stalker

Replace Raid Leader [1] with the following option:

- **Raid Leader [1]** - Gain Aura (Wild Charge (+D3) - Tracker only) and Inspiring for 25 points. This upgrade cannot be combined with magical artefacts.

Gakamak [1]

Amend Nerve value to 14/16 and points cost to 220.

New Unit

Ulpgar the Mad [1]						Ht 2
Hero (Hv Inf), Spellcaster (3)						

Sp 5	Me 4+	Unit Size	US	Att	Ne	Pts
		1	0	1	-/12	120
Ra -	De 4+					

Special Rules
Crushing Strength (1), Individual, Inspiring
Ulpgar's Mad Magic: For each friendly core Heavy Infantry Regiment, Heavy Infantry Horde or Heavy Infantry Legion within 6" of Ulpgar, increase the amount of dice rolled with Bane Chant and Fireball by 1, to a maximum bonus of +11.
Magic of The Bloody Knife Tribe: For each successful hit with Bane Chant, the target unit gains Lifeleech (+1) to a maximum of +3, until the start of the next turn.
Spells
Bane Chant (3), Fireball (7)
Keywords: Orc, Prophet

Formation

Molgurk's Mad Mob

Molgurk is a cunning and sly being, even by orc standards. While most other orc Godspeakers will simply use their magic to blast the enemy or whip their forces into a frenzy, Molgurk uses his magic to make sure he has the loudest War Drum in the tribe. Not only does the War Drum embolden the many orcs swarming around him, it also drives the gruesome gores that pull the chariots of the orcs into a frenzy of violence.

- 1 Wardrum with Chariot upgrade (+20 pts)

- 2 Regiments of Gore Chariots (+5 pts per unit)

The War Drum in this formation gains Spellcaster 1 and the Bane Chant (2) spell.

Gruesome Gores: Unless Disordered, all units in the Formation have the Rampage (Melee - D3) and Slayer (Melee - D3) special rules.

Total Formation cost: +30 pts

UNDEAD

Mhorgoth the Faceless

Amend Speed value to 7 and Drain Life value to (7).

Lykanis

Add the following option:

- **Howl of the Wolf [1]** - Gain Aura (Slayer (Melee - D3) - Beast only) for +25 pts.

Skeleton Warriors

Add the following option:

- Exchange shields for two-handed weapons, lowering Defence to 3+ and gaining Crushing Strength (1) for +5/+5/+10 pts.

Wraiths

This unit is now Irregular.

Revenant Cavalry

Amend points costs to 115/180/305 for the Troop, Regiment and Horde respectively.

Vampire Lord

Gain the following option:

- Upgrade with Blood Rage - Lowering Defence to 4+ and gain Crushing Strength (3) and Lifeleech (3) for free. This option cannot be taken with a mount.

Ghoul Ghast

Add the following option:

- Aura (Thunderous Charge (1) - **Cannibal** only) for +20 pts

Soul Reaver Cavalry

Amend points costs to 155/240 for the Troop and Regiment respectively.

Vampire Lord on Undead Dragon

Amend points cost to 305.

Revenant on Undead Great Burrowing Wyrm

Amend points cost to 200.

Liche King

Replace Drain Life spell option with: Drain Life (6) for 30 points.

Necromancer

Replace Drain Life spell option with: Drain Life (4) for +20 pts.

Revenant King on Undead Great Flying Wyrm

Amend Nerve value to -/18 and points cost to 265

Lady Illona [1]

Amend points cost to 250.

New Unit

Zuinok Iceblood [1]
Hero (Hv Inf), Spellcaster (2)

		Unit Size	US	Att	Ne	Pts	Ht 2
Sp 5	Me 4+	1	0	1	-/13	120	
Ra -	De 5+						

Special Rules
Individual, Inspiring

The Outsider: When Ziunok is included in an Undead army, no other Unique Heroes may be included in the army.

Necrofire: Once per turn, for each point of damage dealt by Ziunok's Fireball spell, Ziunok may immediately remove one point of previously suffered damage on a single Friendly Core **Skeleton** unit without the **Revenant** keyword anywhere within 12" of himself regardless of Line of Sight.

Witchfire: Zuinok can reroll all to-hit rolls of a natural, unmodified 1 with his Fireball spell.

Spells
Fireball (10), Surge (8), Veil of Shadows (3) [1]

Keywords: Arkosaur, Heretic

Formation

The Shambling Blight

When the monstrosity known as a Goreblight is formed, there is a risk that too much dark magic is pumped into a necromancer's creation. These beings, over-saturated with necromantic corruption attract the recently dead until there is a great roaming herd of zombies that is so densely packed, even the most powerful of necromancers will struggle to control the mob.

- 2 Legions of Zombies (+10 pts per unit)

- 1 Goreblight (+5 pts)

All units in this Formation gain the keyword: **The Shambling Blight**. The Zombie Legions in this formation gain the Iron Resolve and Phalanx special rules. The Goreblight in this formation gains the Rallying (1 - **The Shambling Blight**) special rule.

Total Formation cost: +25 pts

ORDER OF THE GREEN LADY

Vial of Sacred Water

Amend the cost of this option to 5 points and the removed damage component to D2 instead of D3.

Add the following units from the Master List: Centaur Bray Hunters.

Naiad Heartpiercers

This unit is no longer Irregular.

Order of the Forsaken

This unit is no longer Irregular. Replace Thunderous Charge (2) with Crushing Strength (1) and Thunderous Charge (1).

Devoted

Remove the [1] limit on Radiance of Life (**Sacred Water** only).

Add the following unique special rule:

Channel the Sacred Water: While within 6" of a Friendly Core **Waterbound** unit, this spellcaster adds 6" to the range of its Bane Chant, Heal, Icy Breath, and Surge spells.

Add the following spell option:

Bane Chant (2) for 20 points.

Order of Redemption

Replace Thunderous Charge (2) with Crushing Strength (1) and Thunderous Charge (1). The unit sizes should be Troop (5) and Regiment (10).

Formation

The Lurkers in the Lake

Summoned in times of great need, the spirits and elementals that slumber in the deep pools of the forests are quick to anger, and harder to stop.

- 2 Hordes of Water Elementals (+5 pts per unit)
- 1 Greater Water Elemental (+5 pts)
- 1 Devoted (+25 pts)

All units in the Formation gain the Wild Charge (1) special rule. The Devoted in this formation gains Inspiring and Aura (Thunderous Charge (+1) - Waterbound only) special rules.

Total Formation cost: +40 pts

Order of Brotherhood on Foot

Add the following option:

Exchange shields for two-handed weapons, lowering Defence to 4+ and gaining Crushing Strength (1) for free.

Greater Water Elemental

Amend Attacks to 9 and Regeneration to (4+).

Add the following option:

- Radiance of Life (**Sacred Water** only) for 15 points.

New Units

Order of the Thorn
Infantry — Ht 2

Sp 5	Me 3+	Unit Size	US	Att	Ne	Pts
Ra -	De 5+	Troop (10)	1	12	11/13	110
		Regiment (20)	3	15	15/17	170

Special Rules
Headstrong, Phalanx
Options
- Vial of Sacred Water for +5 pts
Keywords: Human, Order

Brotherhood Centaurs
Cavalry — Ht 3

Sp 8	Me 3+	Unit Size	US	Att	Ne	Pts
Ra -	De 4+	Troop (5)	1	6	11/13	105
		Regiment (10)	3	12	14/16	160

Special Rules
Crushing Strength (1), Pathfinder, Thunderous Charge (1)
Options
- Vial of Sacred Water for +5 pts
Keywords: Centaur

Champion of the Green Lady [1]
Hero (Cav) — Ht 3

Sp 8	Me 3+	Unit Size	US	Att	Ne	Pts
Ra -	De 5+	1	0	7	-/15	210

Special Rules
Crushing Strength (2), Individual, Inspiring, Mighty, Rallying (1 – Sacred Water only), Regeneration (4+), Strider
Keywords: Human, Sacred Water, Verdant

Order of the Brothermark

The following units gain the Villein keyword. Men-at-Arms Swordsmen, Men-at-Arms Spearmen and Men-at-Arms Crossbowmen.

Villein Penitents

This unit is no longer Irregular. Amend points cost to 75/125/190 for the Regiment, Horde and Legion respectively.

Villein Skirmishers

Add the following option:

- Upgrade to Initiates of the Brothermark (Regiments only)
  - Increase Melee value to 3+ and Waver and Rout values by +1 for +20 pts.

Profile Replacements

Order of the Abyssal Hunt
Cavalry

Sp	Me	Unit Size	US	Att	Ne	Pts	Ht
8	3+	Troop (5)	1	8	12/14	155	3
Ra	De	Regiment (10)	3	16	15/17	235	
-	5+						

Special Rules
Crushing Strength (1), Fury, Iron Resolve, Thunderous Charge (1), Vicious, Slayer (Melee - D3)
Keywords: Human, Order, Tracker

Exemplar Hunter
Hero (Inf)

Sp	Me	Unit Size	US	Att	Ne	Pts	Ht
5	3+	1	0	5	12/14	115	2
Ra	De						
-	5+						

Special Rules
Elite (Melee), Crushing Strength (2), Individual, Iron Resolve, Inspiring (self), Mighty, Slayer (Melee - D3)
Options
- Mount on a Horse, increasing Speed to 8 and changing to Hero (Cav – Height 3) for +35 pts
- The Gauntlet for +10pts

May choose one of the following Orders:
Order of the Bear: Replace Slayer (Melee - D3) with Slayer (Melee - D6) for +15 pts. This option cannot be taken with a mount.
Order of the Lone Wolf: Replace Slayer (Melee - D3) with Rampage (Melee - D3) and gain Pathfinder, Scout, and increase Speed to 6 for +10 pts. This option cannot be taken with a mount.
Order of the Hawk: Gain Ra 4+, Slayer (Ranged - D3) and Silver Crossbow: 18", Piercing (1) for +25 pts. This option cannot be taken with a mount.
Keywords: Human, Paladin, Order, Tracker

New Units

The following profile replaces Paladin Footguard for this army.

Paladin Monster Slayers

Infantry

Ht 2

Sp 5	Me 3+	Unit Size	US	Att	Ne	Pts
Ra -	De 5+	Troop (10)	1	10	11/13	100
		Regiment (20)	3	12	15/17	155
		Horde (40)	4	25	22/24	255

Special Rules
Fury, Iron Resolve, Vicious (Melee - Monsters & Titans only)

Options
Exchange shields for two-handed weapons, lowering Defence to 4+ and increasing Crushing Strength to (1) for free.

Keywords: Human, Order, Paladin

High Chaplain Augustus [1]

Hero (Inf), Spellcaster: 2

Ht 2

Sp 5	Me 3+	Unit Size	US	Att	Ne	Pts
Ra -	De 5+	1	0	4	13/15	145

Special Rules
Crushing Strength (1), Elite (Melee), Individual, Iron Resolve, Inspiring, Mighty, Rally (1 - Human only)

Spells
Heal (5), Bane Chant (3)

Keywords: Human, Paladin

Oathsworn Guardians [1]

Infantry

Ht 2

Sp 5	Me 3+	Unit Size	US	Att	Ne	Pts
Ra -	De 4+	Regiment (20)	3	12	-/17	180

Special Rules
Crushing Strength (1), Duelist, Elite (melee), Inspiring, Iron Resolve, Rampage (D3)

Keywords: Human, Order, Paladin

Formation

Defenders of Righteousness

Life on the frontier is harsh and unforgiving. It takes a certain character with both the physical and mental fortitude to cope with the relentless threat from the hordes of the Abyss. Sir Roderick is one such character and a stalwart of the thin line defending civilisation. Sir Roderick believes that attack is the best form of defence and so, rather than sit behind his castle walls, he is always scouting the hellish landscapes that surround the great scar in the earth, hunting his foes. Whether he's running from something, and trying to banish his own demons, as well as those that emerge from the depths of the Abyss, is unknown, and none dare ask.

- Sir Roderick Demonbane (One High Paladin on Dragon) (+40 pts)

- The Defenders of Righteousness (Two Regiments of Paladin Knights) (+5 pts per unit)

All units in this Formation gain the Brutal special rule. Sir Roderick gains the Cloak of Death special rule.

Total Formation cost: +50 pts

FREE DWARFS

The following units gain the Wild Charge (1) special rule: Free Dwarf Shield Breakers, Free Dwarf Ironwatch Crossbows, Free Dwarf Ironwatch Rifles, Free Dwarf Spear Levy and Free Dwarf Lord.

Berserkers

Remove the option to take Berserkers from the master list (it is replaced with Free Dwarf Berserkers).

Free Dwarf Shieldbreakers

Remove the Scout special rule. Amend points cost to 85/130/215 for Troops, Regiments and Hordes respectively. Add the following option:

- Gain Scout for [+5/+10/+15] pts.

Free Dwarf Brock Riders

Add the following option:

- Gain Pathfinder for [+10/+15] pts

Free Dwarf Spear Levy

Gains the Scout special rule and is no longer Irregular.

Free Dwarf Ironwatch Rifles & Free Dwarf Ironwatch Crossbows

Amend Melee value to 4+ and Unit Strength to 1/3/4 for the Troops, Regiment and Horde respectively.

Herneas the Hunter

Amend points cost to 135.

Free Dwarf Stone Priest

Add the following option:

- Alchemist Curse [1] (3) for 30 pts or free if exchanged for Surge (8).

New Units

Free Dwarf Berserkers
Infantry — Ht 2

Sp	Me	Unit Size	US	Att	Ne	Pts
5	4+	Troop (10)	1	15	-/13	105
Ra	De	Regiment (20)	3	20	-/17	165
-	4+					

Special Rules
Wild Charge (D3), Vicious (Melee), Thunderous Charge (1), Slayer (Melee - D6)
Vengeance: While Counter Charging, this unit has Crushing Strength (+1)
Options
- May gain the Pathfinder special rule for [10/15] pts
Keywords: Berserker, Dwarf

Banick Kholearm [1]
Hero (Inf), Spellcaster: 1 — Ht 2

Sp	Me	Unit Size	US	Att	Ne	Pts
5	4+	1	0	6	12/14	135
Ra	De					
-	5+					

Special Rules
Brutal (1), Crushing Strength (2), Headstrong, Individual, Inspiring, Pathfinder, Scout
Forgeblessed: This unit's Fireball spell always hits on a 4+ regardless of any other modifiers.
Spells
Bane Chant (2), Fireball (10)
Keywords: Dwarf, Flamesmith

Formation

Eryc's Mallets

Eryc and his band of brothers, affectionately known as "The Mallets", have been fighting a guerrilla war deep in the Halpi Mountains, striking out ahead of the forces of Sveri Egilax and in co-ordinated operations with the forces led by Herneas.

- Eryc the Bold (One Free Dwarf Lord) (+10 pts)

- Eryc's Mallets (Three Regiments of Shieldbreakers with the Scout upgrade) (+10 pts per unit)

The Free Dwarf Lord in this formation gains both the Scout and Brutal special rules. The Shieldbreaker Regiments in this formation gain both the Nimble and Brutal special rules. The Shieldbreakers must purchase the Scout upgrade.

Total Formation cost: +40 pts

SALAMANDERS

Scorchwings

Amend Attacks to 7/14 for the Regiment and Horde respectively, and Defence value to 4+.

Ghekkotah Skylord on Scorchwing

Gains the Thunderous Charge (1) and Pathfinder special rules.

Ghekkotah Slasher

Amend Attacks to 10.

Add the following option:

- **Thunderous Drums [1]** - Gain Rallying (1 - **Ghekkotah** only) for +15 pts.

Ghekkotah Hunters

This unit is no longer Irregular. Gains the Steady Aim special rule to both Blowpipes and Bows ranged weapons.

Greater Fire Elemental

Amend Melee value to 3+.

Add the following option:

- Aura (Wild Charge (+1 - Salamanders only)) for 10 pts

Komodons

Gains the Ignores Cover special rule.

Firebrand

Add the following unique special rule:

Crew of Ember's Dance. In an army that contains Firebrand, Corsairs are no longer Irregular.

Clan Lord on Fire Drake

Amend points cost to 290.

New Unit

Rakawas, the Pale Rider [1]						**Ht** 6
Hero (Ttn)						
Sp 6	**Me** 3+	**Unit Size**	**US**	**Att**	**Ne**	**Pts**
Ra 4+	**De** 5+	1	1	12	18/20	245

Special Rules
Crushing Strength (2), Nimble, Inspiring, Vicious
Firebreath: 12", Steady Aim
Keywords: Flamebound, Reptilian, Salamander, Ancient

Formation

The Whispering Scales

The deeds of The Whispering Scales are often lost among the more visible exploits of the Salamander armies. Cutting the lines of ballistae, destroying key supplies, and taking valuable ground before the battlelines form, the Whispering Scales operate in the shadows and strike hard. Seen as distant and detached by their hot-headed brethren, the band keeps to their own and has utmost loyalty to their commander, Zoelkifli the Unseen.

- The Whispering Scales (Two Regiments of Salamander Primes) (+10 pts per unit)

- Zoelkifli the Unseen (One Battle Captain with the Path of Fire [1] upgrade)

All units in this Formation gain the keyword: Whispering Scales and both the Scout and Stealthy special rules. The Battle Captain in this formation gains both the Inspiring and Aura (Elite - Whispering Scales only) special rules.

Total Formation cost: +20 pts

Sylvan Kin

A second Master List is added for the theme: Forces of Nature.

The following additional units can now be taken in a Sylvan Kin army from the Master Lists: Kindred Warriors (Elves), Air Elementals (Forces of Nature), Greater Air Elemental (Forces of Nature) and Woodland Critters (Forces of Nature).

Kindred Gladestalkers

Remove this unit (it is replaced with Sylvan Gladestalkers).

Stormwind Cavalry* (via the Master List)

Add the following option:

- Gain the Pathfinder special rule for [+10/+15] pts.

Forest Shamblers (via the Master List)

Add the following option:

- **Awakened Guardians [1]** (Horde only) - Gain Elite (Melee) and Rallying (1 - **Elf** only) special rules for +20 pts.

Boskwraiths

Gains the Pathfinder special rule.

Hunters of the Wild

Amend points cost to 90/140.

Archwraith

Gains the Pathfinder special rule. Amend Defence value to 4+ and add the following option:

- Aura (Thunderous Charge (+1) - **Boskwraith** only) [1], for 20 pts

Elven King (via the Master List)

Add the following option:

- Wanderer: May be upgraded to a Wanderer, lowering Defence to 4+, increasing both Speed and Attacks to 7 and gaining Pathfinder. This may not be taken with a mount.

Elrik Nisleen

Wayfire. Amend this rule to read; "This unit's Fireball spell always hits a 4+ regardless of any other modifiers".

Tree Herder

Add the following option:

- Upgrade to **The Wiltfather [1]** - Losing Radiance of Life, Increasing Attacks to 10 and its Rout Nerve value by +1 and gaining both Aura (Vicious - Verdant only) and Cloak of Death for +40 pts. This upgrade cannot be taken in addition to a magical artefact.

Avatar of the Green Lady

Amend points cost to 150. Gains the Pathfinder special rule.

New Units

Sylvan Gladestalkers

Infantry

Sp 6	Me 4+	
Ra 4+	De 3+	Ht 2

Unit Size	US	Att	Ne	Pts
Troop (10)	1	10	10/12	130
Regiment (20)	3	12	14/16	175

Special Rules
Elite, Pathfinder, Scout, Steady Aim, Stealthy
Bows: 24"

Options
Deathroot Arrows for +5 pts

Keywords: Elf, Kindred, Tracker

Nimue Waydancer [1]

Hero (Inf), Spellcaster (1)

Sp 6	Me 5+	
Ra -	De 4+	Ht 2

Unit Size	US	Att	Ne	Pts
1	0	1	12/14	150

Special Rules
Cloak of Death, Individual, Inspiring, Stealthy
Wanderer of the Ways: Once per game, before Nimue Waydancer is given an order, she increases her Speed to 10 and gains the Fly special rule until the end of the turn. In the turn this ability is activated, Nimue Waydancer may still cast spells even if she was given an At The Double order.

Spells
Fireball (10), Heal (4), Surge (4), Wind Blast (5)

Keywords: Elf, Verdant

Formation

Wardens of the Sacred Groves

Ar'iana is not royalty. Her bloodline is not that of the great elven kings and queens – far from it. But her feats, wisdom and standing amongst her followers elevates her to such a high status in their eyes, and she puts the survival of the great forests of the world before all else, understanding that they are the heartbeat, lifeblood and soul of the world.

- Ar'iana (One Elven King with the Wanderer upgrade) (+ 5 pts)

- Guardians of the Glade (Two regiments of Forest Guard, Two Troops of Boskwraiths) (+5 pts per unit)

All units gain the Scout special rule

Ar'iana, uses the profile of an Elven King. She gains the Pathfinder and Scout special rules. She must also have the Wanderer upgrade. Both The Wardens of the Groves units gain the Scout special rule.

Total Formation cost: +25 pts

THE HERD

The following additional units can now be taken in The Herd army from the Master List: Hydra and Scorchwings.

Guardian Brutes

Gains the Pathfinder and Brutal special rules, remove the Wild Charge (D3) special rule.

Tribal Trappers

Amend Melee value to 4+.

Chieftain on Minotaur Chariot and Minotaur Chariots.

Amend Speed to 7 and increase Waver Nerve value by +1. Remove the Strider special rule.

Add the following option:

- Upgrade to **The Stampede [1]** (Regiment only) -Gaining both the Strider and Pathfinder special rules and increase its Waver Nerve value by +1 and Rout Nerve value by +1 for +30 pts.

Longhorns

Gains Rallying (1 - Herd only).

Great Chieftain

Amend points cost to 95

Add the following option:

- **Horn of the Great Migration [1]** - Gain Dread and Aura (Wild Charge (+1)) for +15 pts.

New Units

Avatar of the Father [1]
Hero (Mon) — Ht 5

Sp	Me	Unit Size	US	Att	Ne	Pts
10	3+	1	1	9	17/19	285
Ra	De					
-	5+					

Special Rules

Crushing Strength (2), Fly, Fury, Nimble, Pathfinder, Thunderous Charge (1), Very Inspiring

Keywords: Beast, Herd

Flaxhoof [1]
Hero (Cav) — Ht 3

Sp	Me	Unit Size	US	Att	Ne	Pts
8	3+	1	0	6	13/15	160
Ra	De					
-	4+					

Special Rules

Aura (Thunderous Charge (+1) - **Centaur** only), Crushing Strength (2), Fury, Individual, Inspiring, Mighty, Pathfinder

Keywords: Centaur

Formation
The Silent Hunt

Softhoof's tribe have a fearsome reputation as expert ambushers, making vast swathes of forest no-go areas except for the exceptionally brave, or the unsuspecting. Those who venture too close to her domain will find themselves snared by traps and hunted as prey. If you realise you are the target of one of Softhoof's traps, it is already too late.

- Softhoof (Tribal Tracker) (+20 pts)

- Softhoof's Herdkin (Two Regiments of Tribal Trappers) (+5 pts per unit)

All units in this Formation gain the Ensnare special rule. Softhoof's nerve is increased to 11/13 and gains the Aura (Vicious - **Tracker** only) special rule.

Deadly Snares

Whenever a unit from this Formation is touching Difficult Terrain and is attacked in Melee, the attacking unit(s) immediately receives D3 points of damage. No Nerve tests are required for damage caused in this way.

Total Formation cost: +30 pts

KINGDOMS OF MEN

Militia

Amend points cost to 65/105/155 points for the Regiment, Horde and Legion respectively.

Mammoth

Gains the Rampage (Melee - D6) special rule.

Giant

Gains the Slayer (Melee - D6) special rule.

Mounted Scouts

Amend points cost of Blackpowder weapons to [+10/+15] pts.

Fanatic Instigator

Gains the Individual special rule. Add the following option:

- Rallying (1 - **Berserker** only) for +15 pts

New Units

Beast Cavalry
Large Cavalry

Sp	Me	Unit Size	US	Att	Ne	Pts
7	3+	Regiment (3)	2	9	12/14	125
Ra	De	Horde (6)	3	18	15/17	210
-	5+					

Ht 4

Special Rules
Crushing Strength (1)
Options
May choose one of the following options:
- Gain Fly and Speed 10 for [+25/+40] pts
- Gain Thunderous Charge (1) and Vicious for [+10/+20] pts
Keywords: Beast, Human

The Monarch [1]
Hero (Ttn)

Sp	Me	Unit Size	US	Att	Ne	Pts
7	3+	1	1	10	17/19	235
Ra	De					
-	5+					

Ht 6

Special Rules
Crushing Strength (3), Very Inspiring
Options
- Upgrade with Wings, increasing speed to 10 and gaining Fly and Nimble for 50 pts.
May choose one of the following Options:
- **Crown of Chivalry** - Gain Rallying (2 - **Knight** only) for +20 pts
- **Sceptre of Vigor** - Gain Aura (Vicious - **Berserker** only) for +20 pts
- **Sword of Mercy** - Gain Slayer (Melee - 3) for +15 pts
Keywords: Beast, Human

The Brigand [1]
Hero (Inf)

Sp	Me	Unit Size	US	Att	Ne	Pts
5	3+	1	0	4	11/13	75
Ra	De					
4+	4+					

Ht 2

Special Rules
Crushing Strength (1), Individual, Inspiring
Recurve Bow: 24", Piercing (1)
A Merry Band: The Brigand may only be taken as part of the formation: The Outlaws
Keywords: Human, Tracker

Formation

Outlaws

Throughout the realms of men there are always individuals who live their lives outside of the law. Some of these criminals become highly skilled with a bow, and whilst they usually employ these weapons to further their own causes, at times of war they will often band together to shower the enemy with arrows – for enough coin.

- 2 Troops of Bowmen (+5 pts per unit)

- The Brigand [1]

The Bowmen in this Formation gain both the Steady Aim and Volley Fire special rules.

Volley Fire: When issued a Halt order, the unit may choose to have both the Indirect Fire and Ignore Cover special rules for the rest of the Turn.

Total Formation cost: +10 pts

THE LEAGUE OF RHORDIA

Halfling Unit Updates

For halfling units with Relentless, see the halfling army list on page 46.

Duke

Add the following options:

- Rallying (1 - Knights only) for +15 pts

- Swap shield for 2-handed weapon, decreasing Defence to 4+ and gaining Crushing Strength (2) for free. This option may not be taken with a mount.

Profile Replacements

Halfling Braves
Infantry

Sp 5	Me 5+	Unit Size	US	Att	Ne	Pts	Ht 2
Ra -	De 4+	Regiment (20)	2	12	12/14	80	
		Horde (40)	3	25	19/21	130	
		Legion (60)	4	30	25/27	190	

Special Rules
Spellward
Options
- Relentless for +5 pts

Keywords: Halfling, Ravenous

Halfling Knights
Cavalry

Sp 8	Me 3+	Unit Size	US	Att	Ne	Pts	Ht 3
Ra -	De 5+	Troop (5)	1	8	10/12	120	
		Regiment (10)	3	16	13/15	185	
		Horde (20)	4	32	20/22	315	

Special Rules
Nimble, Thunderous Charge (1), Spellward
Options
- Relentless for +5 pts

Keywords: Halfling, Ravenous

Halfling Master Sergeant
Hero (Inf)

Sp 5	Me 3+	Unit Size	US	Att	Ne	Pts	Ht 2
Ra -	De 5+	1	0	3	10/12	55	

Special Rules
Crushing Strength (1), Individual, Inspiring, Spellward
Options
- Mount on a war pony, increasing Speed to 8 and changing to
- Hero (Cav - Height 3) for +25 pts
- Gain Scout for +10 pts. This cannot be in addition to the mount.
- Gain the Ranged attack - Bow: 18", Ra 4+ for +10 pts
- Relentless for +5 pts
- **Loyalist Standard [1]** - This unit gains the Aura (Spellward special rule for +15 pts

Keywords: Halfling, Ravenous

Dogs of War

Infantry

						Ht 2

Sp 5	Me 4+	Unit Size	US	Att	Ne	Pts
Ra -	De 4+	Regiment (20)	3	15	13/15	105
		Horde (40)	4	30	20/22	175

Special Rules

- Indomitable Will for +10 pts

Must choose one of the following options.

- The Shields of Hetronburg [1] - Change Defence to 5+ and gain Phalanx and Ensnare for [+50/+90] pts
- The Razors of Berlonviche [1] - Change Melee to 3+, gain Phalanx and Elite for [+45/+75] pts
- Beasts of Targun Spire [1] - Gain Crushing Strength (1), Fury, and Pathfinder for [+30/+50] pts

Keywords: Human, Mercenaries

New Units

Duke Hetronburg [1]

Hero (Lrg Cav)

						Ht 4

Sp 8	Me 3+	Unit Size	US	Att	Ne	Pts
Ra -	De 5+	1	1	5	14/16	175

Special Rules

Crushing Strength (2), Iron Resolve, Nimble, Rallying (2 - Cavalry only), Thunderous Charge (1), Very Inspiring

Keywords: Aralez, Human

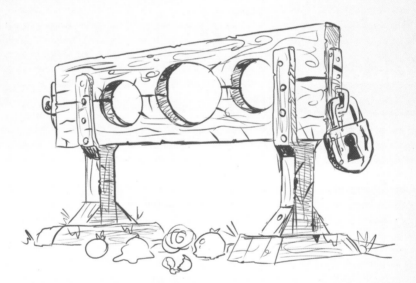

Formation

The Loyalists

When the halflings seceded from the League, not all of them wished for self-rule. Some halflings who have lived in human cities for generations, felt more kinship with the humans, even as anti-halfling rhetoric increased. Others saw the practicality of staying with a large military power, or saw their own economic interests soar as halfling cuisine became a delicacy. Master Sergeant Tory Chalmbler was a staunch supporter of re-unification and soon became the poster-boy for the League's propaganda machine.

- Loyalist Infantry (Two Hordes of Halfling Braves) (+10 pts per unit)

- Loyalist Knights (Two Troops of Halfling Knights) (+5 pts per unit)

- Master Sergeant Tory Chalmbler (One Halfling Master Sergeant) (+20 pts)

All units in this Formation gain the Iron Resolve and Headstrong special rules. The Halfling Master Sergeant in this formation gains the Aura (Elite (Melee) - **Halfling** only) special rule.

Total Formation cost: +50 pts

RATKIN

Death Engine Impaler

Gains the Wild Charge (D3) and Rampage (Melee - D6) special rules.

Scurriers

Amend Melee value to 3+.

Shredder

Amend Attacks to 4.

Nightmares

Amend Vicious (melee) to Vicious.

Hackpaws

Add the following option:

- Plague Pots for +15 pts.

Shock Troops

Amend Heavy Halberds option point cost to [+10/+15/+25] pts.

Mutant Rat-fiend

Remove Walking Womb keyword. Add the Vermin Spawn unique special rule.

Friendly Core **Vermin** units without the **Abomination** keywords regain (D3) points of previously suffered damage instead of one from this unit's Radiance of Life special rule. The D3 is rolled only once each turn, when this unit is given a move order. This rule does not affect this unit itself.

War Chief

Add the following option:

- Aura (Vicious (Melee) - Infantry only) for +15 pts.

New Units

Twitch Keenear [1]
Hero (Inf), Spellcaster (3)

		Unit Size	US	Att	Ne	Pts	Ht 2
Sp 6	Me 5+	1	0	1	-/12	120	
Ra -	De 4+						

Special Rules
Individual, Inspiring
Eye of the Abyss: If Twitch Keenear successfully casts Bane Chant, the target unit may, after rolling to hit and to damage in the Melee phase, discard all damage caused and start again. Roll to hit and to damage again. The second result stands. Rerolling in this way must take place before testing for Nerve or rolling any other attacks from other units in the same Melee.
Spells
Bane Chant (3), Hex (3)
Keywords: Ratkin

Birthing Daughter
Hero (Inf)

		Unit Size	US	Att	Ne	Pts	Ht 2
Sp 6	Me 5+	1	0	1	10/12	80	
Ra 4+	De 4+						

Special Rules
Aura (Strider - **Expendable** only), Individual, Inspiring
Blight Pistol: 12", Piercing (1), Att: 3
Keywords: Expendable, Ratkin

Formation

Smoke, Mirrors and Death

Whilst it is hypothesised that they gleaned much from their former Abyssal Dwarf masters, quite how the Ratkin build their war engines is a mystery. No two are ever exactly the same. Some horrifying examples seem to appear from nowhere, before unleashing a devastating bombardment on their unsuspecting foes - some wicked magic and despicable blightcraft is no doubt at play.

- 2 Shredders (+5 pts per unit)
- 1 Death Engine Spewer (+25 pts)

The Death Engine Spewer gains the Aura (Iron Resolve - Tek only), Inspiring, and Steady Aim special rules. You may redeploy any of the units from this Formation after deployment from both players is finished, but before Scout moves are made.

Total Formation cost: +35 pts

Ratkin Slaves

The Last Breath

The text of The Last Breath rule should read:

When the unit suffers a Rout result, all units in base contact with it suffer 2D3 hits at Piercing (2). These hits are resolved by the player that Routed the unit with The Last Breath rule, which now has to (grudgingly, we're sure) resolve the hits against their own unit(s). After the damage has been resolved, no Nerve test is taken by the damaged units and they proceed to Regroup as normal. In addition, a unit with The Last Breath upgrade cannot take the Crystal Pendant of Retribution magical artefact.

Slave Death Engine Impaler

Gains the Wild Charge (D3) and Rampage (Melee - D6) special rules.

Taskmaster on Chariot

Amend Melee value to 3+ and gain Rallying (1 - **Slaves** only). Remove the option to purchase Rallying (1) for +15 pts.

Slave Warriors

This unit is no longer Irregular.

Slave Nightmares

Amend Vicious (Melee) to Vicious.

Golekh Skinflayer

Amend Attacks to 7.

New Unit

Cryza's Gore-Impaler [1]						Ht 5
Hero (Mon-Cht)						

Sp 8	Me 3+	Unit Size	US	Att	Ne	Pts
		1	0	D6+7	-/16	210
Ra -	De 5+					

Special Rules

Battering Ram, Crushing Strength (2), Rampage (Melee - D6), Vicious (Melee), Wild Charge (D3)

Battering Ram: Once per turn, when this unit routs an enemy unit in melee which has a Unit Strength of 1 or more, it can Overrun as if it had routed an individual.

(See Overrun on pg. 34 of the Rulebook & pg. 30 of the Gamer's Edition). **Note:** Base size cannot be increased beyond 50x100mm

Keywords: Ratkin, Slave, Tek

Formation

Lowest of the Low

An Abyssal Dwarf adage is that "there are plenty more where they came from". The ruthless Taskmasters are not afraid to demonstrate this with callous but tactical wholesale executions of their army's own units.

- 1 Taskmaster on Chariot (+35 pts)

- 1 Horde and 2 Regiments of Slave Warriors, all with the Last Breath upgrade.

The Taskmaster on Chariot increases its Nerve to 13/15, gains the Aura (Vicious (Melee) - Slave Infantry only) and Out of my way, worm! special rules.

Out of my way, worm!: Before giving this unit an order, select a single Friendly Core unit with the Slave keyword within 12" and in Line of Sight of this unit. That unit is then immediately Routed and removed from the board. If the removed unit had the Last Breath upgrade, it activates as normal against all units Engaged with it.

Total Formation cost: +35 pts

TWILIGHT KIN

Impalers

Gains the Fury special rule. Amend points cost to 105/165 for the Troop and Regiment respectively.

Blade Dancers

Amend points cost to 125/190 for the Troop and Regiment respectively.

Butchers

Gains the Fury special rule. Amend Nerve value to 13/15 and 16/18 on the Regiment and Horde respectively.

Summoner Crone

Replace the Sceptre of Shadows upgrade with:

- **Sceptre of Shadows [1]** - This unit's Wicked Miasma unique special rule also affects Friendly Core units with the Elf keyword for +10 pts.

Mikayel

Amend points cost to 230.

Cronebound Shadowhounds

Amend Speed to 10.

Shadowhulk

Gains the Slayer (Melee - D3) special rule.

Cronebound Banshee

Amend Ht to 2.

Profile Replacements

Cronebound Archfiend
Hero (Ttn), Spellcaster: 0

Sp	Me	Unit Size	US	Att	Ne	Pts
10	3+	1	1	9	17/19	305
Ra	De					
-	5+					

Ht 6

Special Rules
Brutal, Crushing Strength (3), Fly, Inspiring, Nimble, Stealthy, Vicious (Melee)
Spells
Fireball (10)
Keywords: Abyssal, Cronebound

New Units

Blade Dancer Neophytes
Infantry

Sp	Me	Unit Size	US	Att	Ne	Pts
6	3+	Troop (10)	1	10	10/12	80
Ra	De	Regiment (20)	3	12	14/16	120
-	3+	Horde (40)	4	25	21/23	200

Ht 2

Special Rules
Elite (Melee)
Keywords: Elf, Neophyte

The following profile replaces Kindred Gladestalkers for this army.

Twilight Gladestalkers
Infantry

Sp	Me	Unit Size	US	Att	Ne	Pts
6	3+	Troop (10)	1	10	10/12	130
Ra	De	Regiment (20)	3	12	14/16	175
4+	3+					

Ht 2

Special Rules
Elite, Pathfinder, Scout
Bows: 24"
Dreamslayer Venom: This unit's melee attacks always damage the enemy on a 4+ regardless of any other modifiers.
Keywords: Elf, Kindred, Tracker

Soulbane on Dread-fiend
Hero (Lrg Cav)

Sp	Me	Unit Size	US	Att	Ne	Pts
8	3+	1	1	6	14/16	165
Ra	De					
-	5+					

Ht 4

Special Rules
Crushing Strength (2), Dread, Elite (Melee), Inspiring, Nimble, Stealthy
Options
Screamshard for +5 pts
Keywords: Cronebound, Elf, Twilight

La'theal Bleakheart [1]
Hero (Inf), Spellcaster: 3

		Unit Size	US	Att	Ne	Pts	Ht
Sp 6	**Me** 5+	1	1	4	13/15	165	2
Ra -	**De** 4+						

Special Rules
Aura (Stealthy), Individual, Inspiring

Wicked Miasma: See Summoner Crone.

The Eye of Valak: At the start of each friendly Ranged phase, if La'theal is not Disordered, she may select an enemy unit within 12" regardless of Line of Sight. This unit loses Stealthy and Spellward until the end of the Turn. All spells targeting this unit may re-roll all natural unmodified to-hit rolls of a 1 until the end of the Turn.

Spells
Drain Life (7), Fireball (10)

Keywords: Elf, Twilight

Formation

The Crew of the Black Hydra

At sea, Leiz's reputation as a pirate is near legendary. A terror of the Infant Sea, his cutthroat crew are fanatical to his cause. To hone their skills while their vessel the Black Hydra undergoes repairs, they will often join their brethren on land in whatever blood thirsty crusade Leiz's peers are waging. There's a price of course for Leiz's help – and woe betide those that do not pay it.

- Leiz the Soulless (one Soulbane) (+15 pts)

- The Soulless Shards (one Regiment and two Troops of Blade Dancers) (+5 pts per unit)

All units in this Formation gain the keyword: The Soulless Shards and the Wild Charge (1) special rule. Leiz gains the Rallying (1 - **The Soulless Shards**) special rule, lowers his Defence to 4+ and increases both his Speed and Attacks to 7. He also may not take a mount.

Enraged: In addition to their basic attacks, each unit in this Formation gains a number of additional attacks equal to their current points of Damage.

Total Formation cost: +25 pts

VARANGUR

The following units from the master list gain the Bloodbound keyword: Human Clansmen, Huscarls, Frostfang Cavalry, Lord on Frostfang, Thegn on Frostfang, Skald and Lord on Chimera.

Reavers

Gains the Wild Charge (D3) special rule.

Amend the Mask of the Reaper option to:

- Upgrade with a Mask of the Reaper, gaining Lifeleech (2) for [+5/+10] pts

Night Raiders

This unit is no longer Irregular and no longer has Scout. Amend Range value to 4+.

Amend the Wolf Handlers option to:

- Wolf Handlers [3]: Gain Aura (Vicious (Melee) - **Tundra Wolf** only) and Scout for +15 pts.

Fallen

This unit is no longer Irregular.

Lord

Amend Attacks to 6. Add the following options:

- **Devoted Icon [1]** - You may choose one of the following upgrades for +20 pts - this may not be taken with a mount:
  - Icon of the Warrior: Aura (Brutal (+1) - **Barbarian** only)
  - Icon of the Reaper: Aura (Lifeleech (+1) - **Barbarian**
  - only)
  - Icon of the Deceiver: Aura (Stealthy - **Barbarian** only)
- Mount on a horse, losing Wild Charge (1) but increasing Speed to 8 and changing to Hero (Cav - Height 3) for +35 pts

New Unit

Kruufnir [1]
Hero (Mon Inf)

							Ht 3

Sp	Me	Unit Size	US	Att	Ne	Pts
6	3+	1	1	5	14/16	160

Ra	De
-	5+

Special Rules

Crushing Strength (2), Nimble, Rampage (3), Regeneration (5+), Very Inspiring, Vicious (Melee), Wild Charge (D3)

Bring me their Head: At the start of the Melee phase, choose a Friendly Core **Bloodbound** unit within 12" of this unit regardless of Line of Sight. That unit gains Duelist until the end of the Turn.

Keywords: Troll, Bloodbound

Formation

Sliksneer's Shriekers

It is said that the horse raiders of the Mammoth Steppes are born at a gallop. No one has seen the nomadic tribes set up camp, but plenty have been able to coax their warriors to their cause with promises of loot and plunder. Sliksneer's Shriekers are among the most feared, charging into battle with a warcry that is said to make a skeleton's bones rattle.

- Mammoth Steppe Horse Raiders (Two Horse Raider Regiments) (+10 pts per unit)
- Sliksneer (Lord on horse with the Icon of the Warrior upgrade)

The Horse Raiders gain Melee 3+. The Lord has a horse and the Icon of the Warrior options despite the normal restriction.

Total Formation cost: +20 pts